DATE			

JUN - - 2022

INTERNET FOR THE PEOPLE

INTERNET FOR THE PEOPLE

The Fight for Our Digital Future

Ben Tarnoff

VERSO

London • New York

First published by Verso 2022
© Ben Tarnoff 2022

1 3 5 7 9 10 8 6 4 2

Verso
UK: 6 Meard Street, London W1F 0EG
US: 388 Atlantic Avenue, Brooklyn, NY 11217
versobooks.com

Verso is the imprint of New Left Books

ISBN-13: 978-1-83976-202-4
ISBN-13: 978-1-83976-203-1 (UK EBK)
ISBN-13: 978-1-83976-204-8 (US EBK)

British Library Cataloguing in Publication Data
A catalogue record for this book is available from the British Library

Library of Congress Cataloging-in-Publication Data

Names: Tarnoff, Ben, author.
Title: Internet for the people : the fight for our digital future / Ben
Tarnoff.
Description: London ; New York : Verso, 2022. | Includes bibliographical
references and index.
Identifiers: LCCN 2021053057 (print) | LCCN 2021053058 (ebook) | ISBN
9781839762024 (hardback) | ISBN 9781839762048 (ebk)
Subjects: LCSH: Internet industry—United States. | Internet—Government
policy—United States. | Internet—Political aspects—United States. |
Democracy—United States.
Classification: LCC HD9696.8.U62 T37 2022 (print) | LCC HD9696.8.U62
(ebook) | DDC 338.7/61025040973—dc23/eng/20220111
LC record available at https://lccn.loc.gov/2021053057
LC ebook record available at https://lccn.loc.gov/2021053058

Typeset in Garamond by Biblichor Ltd, Edinburgh
Printed and bound by CPI Group (UK) Ltd, Croydon CR0 4YY

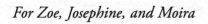
For Zoe, Josephine, and Moira

Contents

Preface

Among the Eels

At the bottom of the ocean there is a garden hose stuffed with glass. Life is difficult at this depth. The lack of light means there is no photosynthesis. Plants are unknown; oxygen is scarce. There are fish with very large eyes and fish that glow. There are octopi with no ink and eels with very large mouths. All these creatures have to eat is each other, and the nutrients on the ocean floor. In this inhospitable place, miles undersea, they have found a way to make a world.

Their world may seem strange, but it has a point of contact with our own. That hose filled with glass is ours; we put it there. It is a bundle of optical fibers that carry beams of light. The beams of light are bits of data, encoded as pulses. The bits of data are Facebook friend requests and financial trades, Twitch streams and supply chain analytics. They flow to and from the internet, irrigating the billions of computers that coordinate the global economy and, increasingly, our everyday lives. Here, among the eels, lies a major artery of the algorithmic age.

There are many such arteries, traversing oceans and tracking continental coastlines, but this one is known as MAREA. It is currently the highest-capacity submarine fiber-optic cable in the world. It is co-owned by Microsoft, Facebook, and a subsidiary of the Spanish telecom Telefónica, which has leased a portion of its capacity to Amazon. The cable reaches a depth of more than seventeen thousand feet and spans more than four thousand miles. It crosses the Atlantic, running from a suburb of Bilbao, Spain, to Virginia Beach in the United States. Where it comes ashore, it looks like a snake rising out of the sea.

MAREA is a reminder that the internet has a body. A body of glass, copper, silicon, and a thousand other things—things that have to be dug out of the earth and hammered into useful shapes, with significant inputs of labor and energy. Bodies are material; they are also historical. If the internet is not a place of pure spirit—a "civilization of the Mind," as the cyberlibertarian John Perry Barlow once called it—neither is it a place untouched by the past. It is entangled with history, and often in quite literal ways.

One way is infrastructural. Submarine cables like MAREA, writes the scholar Nicole Starosielski, frequently follow "the contours of earlier networks." Installing underwater lines is expensive, and it's safer to follow known paths than to pioneer new ones. As a result, the fiber-optic cables that run along the seabed often take the same route as their analog ancestors: the telephone networks of the twentieth century and the telegraph networks of the nineteenth.

These earlier networks were built for particular purposes and used for particular ends. The telegraph networks helped the British supervise and secure their colonial holdings. The telephone networks helped the Americans wage the Cold War, and a hot war in Vietnam. Both networks were essential for capitalist expansion and globalization: they aided in the creation of markets, the extraction of resources, the division and distribution of labor. And, as Starosielski explains, they were themselves shaped by even older patterns of empire and capital. Their cables typically shadowed the sea routes pioneered in previous centuries, routes that sped the circulation of cotton, silver, spices, settlers, and slaves.

Connectivity is never neutral. The growth of networks was guided by a desire for power and profit. They were not just conduits for conveying information, but mechanisms for forging relationships of control. While the internet is more sophisticated than its predecessors, it continues this tradition. The internet is not just material and historical, then; it is also political. The submerged threads of glass that link one landmass to another are, to borrow a metaphor from Eduardo Galeano, veins. Through them, wealth is extracted and concentrated, communities are dominated and dispossessed.

This is not a recipe for despair. On the contrary: an internet with a body, enmeshed in the past and in politics, is also an internet made by people. It is steeped in the struggles through which humans make their social worlds. "Progress" or "technology" or some other inevitable logic of development did not prescribe its present form. Particular choices brought us to this point. We have the ability, collectively, to choose differently.

Market Failure

Up on land, where data rises from the depths to find its destination, people are worried about the internet. They worry about fake news, surveillance, censorship, racism, and several other things. They worry that the connectivity furnished by MAREA and the other glass strands encircling the Earth is not only making the world smaller but making it worse.

Since 2016, a mood of distrust has congealed around the large tech companies that dominate the internet. Often called the "techlash," it has become a fixture of US media and politics. The belief that the internet is broken has become a new common sense. The brokenness of the internet is the subject of congressional hearings and *New York Times* investigations, executive orders and popular documentaries. It is something that, in a fractured partisan landscape, nearly everyone can agree on.

If the internet is broken, how do we fix it? The answers that currently predominate among American policymakers and policy intellectuals tend to circle a couple of main themes. Today's internet reformers talk about monopoly power and the lack of regulation. They argue that tech companies are too large and too little constrained by government. They want to make markets more competitive, firms more regulated.

The internet reformers have some good ideas, but they never quite reach the root of the problem. The root is simple: the internet is broken because the internet is a business. While the issues are various and complex, they are inextricable from the fact that the internet is owned by private firms and is run for profit. An internet owned by smaller, more entrepreneurial, more regulated firms will still be an internet run for profit. And an internet run for profit is one that can't guarantee people the things they need to lead self-determined lives. It's an internet where people can't participate in the decisions that affect them. It's an internet in which the rewards flow to the few and the risks are borne by the many. In other words, it's the internet as we know it today.

The internet has not always existed in its current form. It had to be made. This book is about how it was made, and what we can do to change it. It focuses on the United States— a scope that is at once provincial, given the fact that more than 93 percent of internet users now live outside the United States, and reasonable, given the historical and ongoing centrality of American institutions to the internet's existence. In particular, this book is mostly about the internet's privatization, because privatization is the process that made the modern internet. It is also the process that set in motion the crises that have provoked the techlash.

Into the Stack

The internet started out in the 1970s as an experimental technology created by US military researchers. In the 1980s, it grew into a government-owned computer network used primarily by academics. Then, in the 1990s, privatization began. The privatization of the internet was a process, not an event. It did not involve a simple transfer of ownership from the public sector to the private but rather a more complex movement whereby corporations programmed the profit motive into every level of the network. A system built by scientists was renovated for the purpose of profit maximization. This took hardware, software, legislation, entrepreneurship. It took decades. And it touched all of the internet's many pieces.

The internet's pieces don't fit together in an especially obvious way. Most of the infrastructure on which our daily lives depend is easy to visualize: a highway, a power plant. But the internet is too sprawling to squeeze into a single frame. There is no bird's-eye view of the internet. That's why metaphors matter. Some things are too small to see without a microscope; others are too big to see without a metaphor. And one metaphor that is particularly useful for thinking about the internet, and which has guided its architects from the beginning, is the stack.

A stack is a set of layers piled on top of one another. Think of a house: you have the basement, the first floor, the second floor, and so on, all the way up to the roof. The things that you do further up in a house often depend on systems located further down. If you take a shower, a water heater in the basement warms up the cold water being piped into your house and then pipes it up to your bathroom.

The internet also has a basement, and its basement also consists largely of pipes. Some, like MAREA, carry data across oceans; most carry data across shorter distances. There are many different kinds of pipes, of varying length and complexity. Everything you do up the stack depends on these pipes working properly. Up the stack is where the sites and apps live. This is where we experience the internet, through the pixels of our screens, in emails or tweets or streams.

The process of privatization started in the internet's basement, with the pipes. In the 1990s, the US government gave the private sector a network created at enormous public expense. Corporations took over the internet's physical infrastructure and made money from selling access to it. But privatization didn't stop there. The real money didn't lie in monetizing access, but in monetizing activity—that is, in what people did once they got online. So privatization ascended to the upper floors, to the layer where the internet is experienced. Here, in the 2000s and 2010s, the so-called platforms arose: Google, Amazon, Uber, and the rest. These empires finished what the 1990s had started. They pushed privatization up the stack. The profit motive came to organize not only the low-level plumbing of the network but every aspect of online life.

New Directions

This book is not a manifesto in the traditional sense. It is not particularly programmatic, though it does contain some proposals. Rather, it is a manifesto in the sense that it tries to make something manifest, something that so far has not been very visible: the story of the internet's privatization.

Understanding this story, and understanding it as a single story, helps explain the origins of the modern internet and its crises. The techlash is nothing if not a belated reckoning with the legacies of privatization. But if its critiques remain confined to the symptoms and fail to grasp the underlying cause, it won't yield much in the way of meaningful change.

Understanding the story of privatization also helps us see how problems that might seem distinct are actually connected: how severe inequalities in broadband access and the proliferation of right-wing propaganda on social media are in fact two moments of the same movement. Further, it helps us identify the source of those problems. Privatization has a history, and anything with a history can come to an end.

To build a better internet, we need to change how it is owned and organized. Not with an eye toward making markets work better, but toward making them less dominant. Not in order to create a more competitive or more rule-bound version of privatization, but to overturn it.

Deprivatization aims at creating an internet where people, and not profit, rule. This sounds like a protest chant but I mean it quite literally. The people whose lives are most affected by a particular decision should be the ones who have the most say in it. But so long as the internet is controlled by firms that are compelled to prioritize profit-making as a matter of survival—without profit, or the promise of profit, there is no firm—this sort of democratic decision-making can't take place. A small number of executives and investors will continue to make choices on everyone's behalf, and these choices will remain tightly bound by the demands of the market. A democratic internet must be bound by a different set of demands: those that arise from people's desire for self-determination. The satisfaction of such demands requires, among other things, taking collective control of the online spaces where our common life increasingly takes place.

This book presents a few directions for doing so. It calls for shrinking the space of the market and diminishing the power of the profit motive. It calls for developing models of public and cooperative ownership that encode the principles of collective governance and popular participation. But the scale and complexity of the internet mean there is no silver bullet for creating a democratic digital future. It will require much experimentation. It will also require creating new structures that enable such experiments to take place. The outcome of these experiments can't be known in advance, which is why the suggestions in the subsequent pages are necessarily provisional. The precise contours of a democratic internet can only be discovered through a democratic process—through people coming together to build the world they want.

There is plenty of wisdom out there for such discoveries to draw from. There are many organizers and scholars who have thought deeply about digital injustice, and many communities that have acquired valuable expertise on the subject from their own encounters with it. Even so, questions will remain: how to end algorithmic racism, for instance, or the right way to handle content moderation. Liberating the internet from the constraints of the profit motive won't make these questions go away. It will, however, create the conditions in which the answers can be found.

PART I

THE PIPES

1

A People's History of the Internet

On November 22, 1977, a van rolled down the freeway between San Francisco and San Jose. It was boxy and gray, the kind used for deliveries. At a distance it would've looked unremarkable: one of countless cars crawling up and down the peninsula in the rain. But if you'd gotten a closer look, you would've seen something a bit unusual: two large antennas stuck to the roof. This was the first clue. Drawing closer, you might've seen something else through the rear windows: a person typing at a computer terminal. In fact, the whole back of the van was filled with electronics. It looked like the inside of a research lab, the sort you might find in the meticulously landscaped office parks of the surrounding region, a place so crowded with semiconductor companies that it had recently become known as Silicon Valley.

But what made this van special wouldn't be visible no matter how close you came. The van was a node in a network. Not a single network, but a network of networks—an *inter-*network. This internetwork was immense. It spanned land, sea, sky, and space, and stitched together computers from all over the world.

The first computer sat in the back of the van. It transformed the words being typed on the terminal into discrete slices of data called "packets." These packets were encoded as radio waves and transmitted from the van's antennas to repeaters on nearby mountaintops, which amplified them. With this extra boost, they could make it all the way to Menlo Park, where an office building received them.

In Menlo Park, the packets underwent a subtle metamorphosis. They shed their ethereal shape as radio waves and acquired a new form: electrical signals in copper telephone lines. Then they embarked on a long journey, riding those lines all the way to the East Coast before sailing via satellite over the Atlantic Ocean.

The packets touched down in a facility on the outskirts of Oslo. From there they ran to London, then over to England's southwestern edge. Goonhilly Satellite Earth Station was the largest facility of its kind in the world at the time: a cluster of satellite dishes encircled by the bogs and marshes of Cornwall. Here, the packets took flight once again. A dish hurled them some twenty thousand miles up into space, where they bounced off an orbiting satellite and dove back down to earth, landing on the other side of the Atlantic, in a narrow valley that cut through the densely forested foothills of the Alleghenies: Etam Earth Station, West Virginia.

Etam wasn't far from the site of the first skirmish of the Civil War. The young Ambrose Bierce had fought in that battle; he would later remember the region as "an enchanted land," thick with fragrant spruce and fir, and populated with wild pigs that had once feasted on the corpses of his fellow Union soldiers.

Here, the packets returned to fixed lines. They continued northeast, to an office in an old warehouse on the western end of Cambridge, Massachusetts, before bending back across the country toward Los Angeles. This was their final destination: a complex overlooking the palm trees and pleasure craft of Marina del Rey, only four hundred miles south of the van where they had originated.

The packets didn't know their route in advance. But they did know their destination. This was written into each packet, like the address on an envelope. Whenever a packet crossed from one network to the next, a computer called a gateway examined the address and forwarded the packet on to its next stop. This routine was repeated until the data reached Marina del Rey. There, the destination computer sent a note to the computer in the van saying the packet had arrived safely; if this acknowledgment wasn't made, the packet was resent. Eventually, when all of the packets had completed the trip, the machine in Marina del Rey pieced them together and displayed the message they contained.

What was in the packets? What did the message say? Nobody remembers. It doesn't matter. What matters isn't what was said but how. The packets had traveled nearly a hundred thousand miles in about two seconds. They had crossed multiple networks and multiple mediums—radio, satellite, fixed-line—while arriving at their destination completely intact. Computers from across the world had talked to one another, and heard each other perfectly, speaking the new universal language of the internet.

Birth of a Network

The internet is fundamentally a language—a set of rules for how computers should communicate. These rules have to strike a very delicate balance. On the one hand, they have to be strict enough to ensure the reliable transmission of data. On the other, they have to be loose enough to accommodate all the different ways that data might be transmitted. Together, these qualities ensure that data can not only go anywhere, but also get there in one piece.

Think about water: it can be vapor, liquid, or ice, but its chemical composition remains the same. This flexibility is a feature of our natural universe. The language of the internet instills a similar flexibility into our digital universe, turning data into something that can flow across any device, network, and medium—which is the reason a smartphone in São Paulo can download a song from a server in Singapore.

That day in 1977 offered the first real evidence that this language could work at scale. There had been earlier experiments, but never one of such complexity. Pulling it off—and getting to the point where it could even be attempted—took a colossal, and collective, effort. The internet wasn't invented by a lone genius tinkering in a garage. Rather, it involved thousands of individuals engaged in a decades-long act of co-creation. It took collaboration, cross-pollination, and the slow, accretive work of building on earlier breakthroughs to generate new ones. It also took a lot of public money.

Most of the innovation on which Silicon Valley depends comes from government-funded research, for the simple reason that the public sector can afford to take risks that the private sector can't. It's precisely the insulation from market forces that enables the government to finance the long-term scientific labor that ends up producing many of the most profitable inventions. This is particularly true of the internet.

The internet was such an unlikely idea that only decades of public funding and planning could bring it into existence. Not only did the basic technology have to be invented, but the infrastructure had to be built, specialists had to be trained, and contractors had to be staffed, funded, and, in some cases, directly spun off from government agencies. The internet is sometimes compared to the interstate highway system, another major public project. But as the activist Nathan Newman points out, the comparison only makes sense if the government "had first imagined the possibility of cars, subsidized the invention of the auto industry, funded the technology of concrete and tar, and built the whole initial system."

The Cold War provided the pretext for this ambitious undertaking. Nothing loosened the purse strings of American politicians quite like the fear of falling behind the Soviet Union. This fear spiked sharply in 1957, when the Soviets put the first satellite into space. The Sputnik launch produced a genuine sense of crisis in the American establishment, and led to a substantial increase in federal research funding.

One consequence was the creation of the Advanced Research Projects Agency (ARPA), which would later change its name to the Defense Advanced Research Projects Agency (DARPA). DARPA became the R&D arm of the Defense Department.

In the early 1960s, DARPA began investing heavily in computing, installing mainframes at universities and the other research sites where its community of contractors worked. But even for an agency as generously funded as

DARPA, this spending spree wasn't sustainable. In those days, a computer cost millions of dollars. So DARPA came up with a way to share its computing resources more efficiently among its contractors: it built a network.

This network was ARPANET, and it laid the foundation for the internet. First connected in 1969, ARPANET linked computers through an experimental technology called packet-switching, which involved breaking messages down into small chunks, routing them through a maze of switches, and reassembling them on the other end. Today, this is the mechanism that moves data across the internet. At the time, the telecom industry considered it absurdly impractical. Years earlier, the Air Force had tried to persuade AT&T to build such a network, ultimately without success. DARPA even offered ARPANET to AT&T after it was up and running. The agency would've preferred to buy time on the network instead of managing it. Given the chance to acquire the most sophisticated computer network in the world, however, AT&T refused. The executives simply couldn't see the money in it.

Luckily, as it turned out. Under public ownership, ARPANET flourished. Government control gave the network two major advantages. The first was money. DARPA could pour cash into the system without having to worry about profitability. The agency commissioned research from the country's most talented computer scientists at a scale that would've been suicidal for a private corporation. And, just as crucially, DARPA enforced an open-source ethic that encouraged collaboration and experimentation. The contractors who contributed to ARPANET had to share the source code of their creations. This catalyzed scientific creativity, as researchers from a range of different institutions could refine and expand on each other's work without living in fear of intellectual property law.

The most important innovation that resulted was the internet protocol, which first emerged in the mid-1970s. Initially, the protocol was a proposal for how computers should communicate. The proposal was subsequently implemented in software and refined through multiple experiments. This made it possible for ARPANET to evolve into the internet, by providing a common language that let very different networks talk to one another. The language would be open and non-proprietary—a free and universal medium, rather than a patchwork of incompatible commercial dialects.

Under private ownership, such a language could never have been created. Not only would the expense have been too great, the very idea of a free and universal medium cut against the grain of the commercial impulse to lock users into a proprietary ecosystem. It was the absence of the profit motive and the presence of public management that made the invention of the internet possible. Yet the internet would also reflect the institutional imperatives of the particular arm of the government that oversaw its creation: the military.

The Mainframe and the Battlefield

The internet was created to win wars, although not right away. As a "blue sky" research outfit, DARPA had wide latitude in picking its projects, but it still had to develop technologies that might someday be useful for military ends. The internet was no exception. Its champions within the agency made the case that the internet was worth pursuing because it could give American forces an edge. This edge would come from taking computing power out of the lab and into the field.

Picture a Jeep in the jungles of Zaire, or a B-52 miles above North Vietnam. Then imagine these as nodes in a wireless network linked to another network of powerful computers thousands of miles away. This is the dream of a networked military using computing to project American power. This is the dream that produced the internet.

ARPANET had been a major breakthrough. But it had a limitation: it wasn't mobile. The computers on ARPANET were gigantic by today's standards. That might work for DARPA researchers, who could sit at a terminal in Cambridge or Menlo Park—but it did little for soldiers deployed deep in enemy territory. For ARPANET to be useful to forces in the field, it had to be accessible anywhere in the world.

This required doing two things. The first was building a wireless network that could relay packets of data among the widely dispersed cogs of the US war machine by radio or satellite. The second was connecting those wireless networks to ARPANET, so that multimillion-dollar mainframes could serve soldiers in combat. "Internetworking," the scientists called it.

Internetworking was hard. Getting computers to talk to one another—networking—had been challenging enough. But getting networks to talk to one another—inter-networking—posed a whole new set of difficulties, because the networks spoke different idioms. Trying to move data from one to another was like writing a letter in Mandarin to someone who only knows Hungarian and hoping to be understood.

In response, the architects of the internet developed a kind of digital Esperanto: a common language that enabled data to travel across any network. In 1974, two researchers named

Robert Kahn and Vinton Cerf published an early blueprint. Drawing on conversations happening throughout the international networking community, they sketched a design for "a simple but very powerful and flexible protocol": a universal set of rules for how computers should communicate.

These rules would make it possible to weave together a network of networks so versatile and so robust that a soldier in the field could connect to a mainframe halfway across the world. Indeed, the experiments that DARPA conducted to test the new idiom of the internet were designed with exactly this scenario in mind. The first major experiment took place in 1976, linking two networks. The second took place in 1977, featuring the van driving down the Bay Area freeway, flinging packets across the Atlantic, linking three networks.

The design of these experiments reflected a specific military scenario. "What we were simulating was a situation where somebody was in a mobile unit in the field, let's say in Europe, in the middle of some kind of action," Cerf later recalled. The soldiers would be trying to access "some strategic computing asset that was in the United States," possibly while engaging or evading the enemy. The goal, in other words, was to bring the mainframe to the battlefield. The van played the role of the mobile unit. The Bay Area freeway was the battlefield. And it worked: the smaller computer in the mobile unit established a link to a bigger computer many miles away.

The protocol developed by Cerf and Kahn had fulfilled its promise. Eventually, it would evolve into a whole suite of protocols called TCP/IP. Today, TCP/IP is the lingua franca of the internet. It is no exaggeration to say that TCP/IP *is* the internet: without its rules, the world's networks would be a Babel of mutually unintelligible tongues.

This universality was created with a particular end in mind. The internet was designed to run anywhere because the US military is everywhere. Today, it maintains around eight hundred bases in some eighty-five countries around the world. It has hundreds of ships, thousands of planes, and thousands of tanks. The reason the internet can work across any device, network, and medium is because it needed to be as ubiquitous as the military that financed its creation. It needed to be able to knit together a heterogeneous collection of people and machines into a single network of networks, so that a soldier in a Jeep or a pilot in a B-52 could use a computer thousands of miles away.

From Protocol to Place

The internet may have been created as a weapon of empire, but the empire wasn't interested—at least not in the original idea. When the US military did embrace TCP/IP, it wasn't because it wanted to link Jeeps to mainframes. Rather, it had a more mundane requirement: it needed to get the Pentagon's growing assortment of fixed-line networks to start talking to one another.

TCP/IP was the answer. Indeed, when it came to reliable internetwork communication, the protocol "was really the only game in town," Kahn later remembered. In 1983, ARPANET switched over to TCP/IP, which let it interconnect with other military and experimental networks. This new system became known as *the* internet, with ARPANET at its center. The internet was born as a protocol; it would now become a place, one increasingly populated by civilian researchers—trading emails, accessing high-performance computers, collaborating, arguing. While the government created the internet, it was users who made it useful, who made it a place worth visiting.

The internet's usefulness soon led scientists from outside DARPA's select circle of contractors to demand access. In response, the National Science Foundation (NSF)—a US government agency tasked with supporting basic research— undertook a series of initiatives aimed at bringing more people online. These culminated in NSFNET, a program that oversaw the creation of a new national network. This network, which first became operational in 1986, would be the new "backbone" of the internet, an assemblage of cables and computers forming the internet's main artery. It resembled a river: data flowed from one end to another, feeding tributaries, which themselves branched into smaller and smaller streams. These streams served individual users, people who themselves never touched the backbone directly. If they sent data to another part of the internet, it would travel up the chain of tributaries to the backbone, then down another chain, until it reached the stream that served the recipient.

In this model, the river is useless without the tributaries that extend its reach. This is why the NSF, to ensure the broadest possible connectivity, subsidized a number of regional networks that linked universities and other participating institutions to the NSFNET backbone. All this wasn't cheap, but it worked. Scholars Jay P. Kesan and Rajiv C. Shah have estimated that the subsidies to the regional networks, together with the cost of running the NSFNET backbone, came to approximately $160 million. Other public sources, such as state governments and state-supported universities, likely contributed more than $1.6 billion to the development of the internet during this period.

In the 1970s, the government invented the universal language of the internet. In the 1980s, it made this language the basis of a cutting-edge communications system and spent heavily on plugging more people into it. Thanks to this avalanche of public cash, the internet became widely available to American researchers by the end of the 1980s. Then, in the following decade, this internet abruptly died, and a different one appeared—one we would recognize today. The 1990s is when the internet became a business. The government ceded the pipes to a handful of corporations while asking nothing in return.

Open for Business

Privatization didn't come out of nowhere. It was the plan all along. The government reports that guided the creation of NSFNET called for the backbone to eventually pass into private hands, but the internet's surprising popularity pushed the NSF to make the transition sooner than expected.

By the early 1990s, the internet was becoming a victim of its own success. Congestion plagued the backbone, and whenever the NSF upgraded it more people piled on. In 1988, users sent less than a million packets a month. By 1992, they were sending 150 billion. Just as new highways produce more traffic, the NSF's improvements only stoked demand, overloading the system.

Clearly, people liked the internet. And these numbers would've been even higher if the NSF had imposed fewer restrictions on its users. NSFNET's Acceptable Use Policy (AUP) banned commercial traffic, preserving the network for research and education purposes only. The NSF considered this a political necessity, since Congress might cut funding if taxpayer dollars were seen to be subsidizing industry. In practice, the AUP was largely unenforceable, as companies regularly used the NSFNET backbone. More broadly, the private sector had been making money off the internet for a long time, both as contractors and as beneficiaries of software, hardware, infrastructure, and engineering talent developed with public funds.

Still, the AUP did have an effect. By formally excluding commercial activity, it spawned a parallel system of private networks. By the early 1990s, a variety of commercial providers had sprung up across the country, offering online services with no restrictions on the kind of traffic they would carry. Most of these networks traced their origins to government funding, and enlisted DARPA veterans for their technical expertise. But whatever their advantages, the commercial networks were prohibited by the AUP from ferrying commercial content over NSFNET, which inevitably limited their value.

The internet had thrived under public ownership, but it was reaching a breaking point. Skyrocketing demand from researchers strained the system, while the AUP prevented it from reaching an even wider audience. Meanwhile, the commercial networks were eager to expand without restrictions, and capitalize on the growing enthusiasm for the internet.

This enthusiasm was driven in part by the rise of the World Wide Web, which made being online much easier. The early internet was not particularly user-friendly. Text-heavy applications like email predominated, and using them generally required a degree of technical skill. The web offered a new, more intuitive approach: a collection of hyperlinked "pages." What we take for granted now—clicking our way through a chain of content—was revelatory at the time. The web did not replace the internet; it lived within the internet. But over the course of the 1990s, many newcomers would come to know the internet primarily through the web, to the point where people had trouble distinguishing between the two.

The first website went up in 1990; the browser that would popularize the web, Mosaic, appeared three years later. As usual, public money played a leading role. Tim Berners-Lee, the creator of the World Wide Web, worked as a scientist at CERN, the European research organization backed by nearly two dozen member states, while Mosaic was developed at the University of Illinois's National Center for Supercomputing Applications, which had been created by the NSF in the 1980s. And it was under these conditions that NSFNET director Stephen Wolff began to pursue privatization. The first step took place in 1991. A few years earlier, the NSF had awarded the contract for operating its network to a consortium of Michigan universities called Merit, in partnership with IBM and MCI. This group had significantly underbid, sensing a business opportunity. In 1991, they decided to cash in, creating a for-profit subsidiary that started selling commercial access to the NSFNET backbone, with Wolff's blessing.

The move enraged the rest of the nascent networking industry. Companies correctly accused NSF of cutting a backroom deal to grant its contractors a commercial monopoly, and raised enough hell to bring about congressional hearings in 1992. These hearings didn't dispute the desirability of privatization, only its terms. Now that Wolff had put privatization in motion, the other commercial providers simply wanted a piece of the action. One of their chief executives, William Schrader, testified that NSF's actions were akin to "giving a federal park to Kmart."

The solution preferred by Schrader and his fellow executives wasn't to preserve the park, however, but to carve it up into multiple Kmarts. Previously, the NSF had considered restructuring the NSFNET backbone to allow more contractors to run it. By 1993, after the congressional hearings and extensive industry input, the NSF had decided on the more radical step of eliminating the NSFNET backbone altogether. Instead of one national backbone, there would be several, all owned and operated by commercial providers.

The goal was to promote competition by creating a level playing field. More accurately, the field remained tilted, but open to a few more players. If the old architecture of the internet had favored monopoly, the new one would be tailor-made for oligopoly. There weren't that many companies that had consolidated enough infrastructure to operate a backbone—there were five, to be exact. NSF wasn't opening the internet to competition so much as transferring it to a small handful of corporations waiting in the wings. Strikingly, this transfer came with no conditions. There would be no federal oversight of the new internet backbones, and no rules governing how the commercial providers ran their infrastructure. Gone too were the subsidies for the nonprofit regional networks that had brought campuses and communities online in the NSFNET days. Some had already spawned commercial spin-offs; those that hadn't were mostly acquired or went bankrupt.

Finally, on April 30, 1995, the NSF terminated the NSFNET backbone. Within the space of a few short years, the privatization of the internet's pipes was complete.

The Electronic Shopping Mall

What's striking about the privatization of the pipes is how nearly everyone agreed it was the right thing to do. While NSFNET director Wolff led the way, he was acting from a broad ideological consensus. "I had people working for me, and we all agreed this was the way to go," he told the writer Yasha Levine many years later. "There wasn't any conflict there."

During the 1990s, free-market triumphalism, and the deregulatory political climate fostered by Bill Clinton's Democrats and Newt Gingrich's Republicans, framed privatization as both beneficial and inevitable. The collapse of the Soviet Union strengthened this view as the Cold War rationale for more robust public planning disappeared. These factors, alongside the depth of industry influence over the process, guaranteed that privatization would take an especially extreme form.

Yet privatization also had a certain subtlety to it. A casual observer could be forgiven for missing the magnitude of the event. The government didn't literally give the private sector a bunch of cables and computers. The decision to kill the NSFNET backbone ensured no hardware changed hands. The government didn't even own the hardware in the first place: the network had always operated on lines leased from contractors and had always relied on contractors to run the backbone on its behalf, just as ARPANET had. Moreover, the TCP/IP protocols that glued the manifold networks of the internet together were nonproprietary. Anyone could use them, and by the mid-1990s, many companies did.

But the government, having controlled the internet's main artery, had the power to determine what would replace it. By the early 1990s, the internet had clearly outgrown NSFNET, and the existing model was no longer tenable. For the internet to continue its evolution, a new arrangement had to be found. That arrangement could have taken many forms. Rather than exploring them, the government empowered industry to unilaterally dictate the terms of the transition. Naturally, industry insisted that the internet's privatization was a precondition for its popularization—the only options, it seemed, were to preserve the system as a restricted research network or to make it a fully privatized mass medium.

This was a false choice. But industry influence guaranteed that it was the only choice presented. Large sums of money were at stake. The government had spent billions of dollars patiently developing a technology that had finally reached the point where it could serve as the basis for a business, and corporations were determined to reap the rewards. In the 1990s, they scored a victory so complete that it became nearly invisible, and quietly revolutionized the technology that would soon revolutionize the world.

Perhaps nothing illustrates the completeness of that victory better than the saga of Al Gore. Since entering Congress in the 1970s, the Tennessee politician had distinguished himself as an early champion of digital technologies. Cerf and Kahn, the architects of the original internet protocol, would later praise Gore as "the first elected official to grasp the potential of computer communications to have a broader impact than just improving the conduct of science and scholarship." Indeed, Gore directly contributed to the growth of the internet: he introduced the High-Performance Computing and Communications Act of 1991, which helped expand NSFNET.

Though a centrist, Gore believed in industrial policy. He saw the "information superhighway" envisioned by his bill as an investment that would stimulate economic growth and promote national competitiveness—a politically salient issue at a time of widespread concern among US policymakers over the rise of Japan. For the network to perform this function, Gore argued, the government had to ensure the benefits were broadly shared. His internet would thus be a public-private partnership: operated by industry, but under federal oversight.

Yet after Gore entered the White House as Bill Clinton's vice president in 1993, his language began to change. The public part of the public-private partnership gradually disappeared. The journalist Robert Krulwich later reported that, on December 21, 1993, the same day that Gore gave a speech at the National Press Club in Washington, DC, conceding that the internet would be an entirely private system, the Democratic National Committee received $90,000 in contributions from four telecom companies. The next day, another $30,000 rolled in. The idea that the government would play a permanent and significant role in the information superhighway receded; the NSF pushed forward with full privatization. Meanwhile, a top priority of the first Clinton administration would be telecom deregulation, culminating with the Telecommunications Act of 1996.

If a centrist politician in a position of power couldn't secure a modest public foothold in the new internet, there was little hope for more radical and less influential voices. Among these was Senator Daniel Inouye, who introduced a bill in 1994 that would have made telecom companies reserve up to 20 percent of their capacity for "public uses." This capacity would be considered "public property"—the telecoms would have no control over it. And it would be used to offer free access to qualifying organizations, such as libraries, nonprofits, and educational institutions, so long as they provided "educational, informational, cultural, civic, or charitable services directly to the public without charge for such services." Such organizations would also receive funding to support their ability to provide these services. The idea had been the brainchild of the Telecommunications Policy Roundtable, a coalition of unionized workers, consumer activists, computer professionals, and others who, during the telecom policy debates of Clinton's first term, offered a lonely counterpoint to the deregulatory enthusiasm of the era by demanding a "public lane on the information superhighway."

One source of inspiration was public media: Inouye's bill cited the Public Broadcasting Act of 1967, which had created the Corporation for Public Broadcasting to promote noncommercial programming on radio and television. Inouye's notion of a differential fee structure also had ample precedent. The US Postal Service charges different rates for different uses of its network: libraries and periodicals pay less. For much of the country's history, in fact, Congress mandated very cheap or even free postage for newspapers and magazines in order to encourage the broad diffusion of information. And NSFNET's predecessor, the Computer Science Research Network (CSNET), had become financially self-sufficient by charging industry laboratories higher rates for linking them to the internet than its rates for universities. Although the details of Inouye's proposal would've had to be worked out, the fundamentals were feasible, and the principles behind it had a long history. There was also a strong moral case. If anything, a public lane was the minimum of what basic fairness demanded: in exchange for the privilege of making a profit from a system built with public money, telecoms would set aside some of their capacity for organizations that served the public.

The idea didn't get far. Inouye's bill went nowhere. Telecom lobbying ensured the public lane would never be built. The Telecommunications Policy Roundtable made a courageous effort, but it didn't muster the kind of mass mobilization that would've been required to overcome industry opposition. "There should be a national debate about what kind of media system we should have," Jeffrey Chester, the organization's co-founder, told the *New York Times* in 1993. "The debate has been framed so far by a handful of communications giants who have been working overtime to convince the American people that the data highway will be little more than a virtual electronic shopping mall."

Without a social movement, however, the telecoms would continue to dominate the debate. The data highway would become the virtual electronic shopping mall. In 1995, the NSFNET backbone was decommissioned; in 1996, the Telecommunications Act was passed; and in 1997, the Clinton administration released its "Framework for Global Electronic Commerce," formally committing the federal government to a market-dominated internet, one in which "industry self-regulation" would take priority and the state would play a minimal role.

There was nothing in the technical composition of the internet that predetermined this outcome. Any number of measures could have popularized the internet without completely privatizing its pipes. A public lane on the information superhighway was one option; another idea would have been to expand NSFNET's nonprofit regional networks rather than abandoning them. Funded with fees secured from the telecoms, these networks could have enabled the government to guarantee high-speed, low-cost internet access as a universal social right. Such a right could also have been secured by supporting and expanding the "free-nets" that had operated since the 1980s: nonprofit networks that offered local communities free access to the internet, typically through a dial-up modem. Tom Grundner, founder of the famous Cleveland Free-Net that pioneered the model, even tried to launch a "Corporation for Public Cybercasting," which would have sprinkled free-nets across the country with federal money.

But the window of possibility closed. In the absence of a strong popular campaign demanding an alternative, the telecoms prevailed. It was, to put it mildly, a missed opportunity.

2

The Plunder Continues

More than a quarter century has passed since the pipes began to be privatized. In that time, the internet has grown beyond recognition. It has become not just a mass medium but an essential infrastructure, analogous to electricity in the depth of its integration into billions of people's lives. It has also gone global. While the early internet and predecessors like ARPANET had nodes overseas, they remained US-centric systems. By contrast, the internet of today is properly international—it is probably better thought of as a set of linked "internets," each centered on the main digital hegemons: China, Europe, and the United States.

But not everything has changed. When you go into the basement of the US internet and examine the pipes, you find much of the old plumbing intact. The ownership model forged by privatization remains in place: a handful of firms still own everything. In 1995, there were five major backbone providers. Today, there are somewhere around six in the US, depending on how you count. While a long chain of mergers and acquisitions has led to rebranding and reorganization, most of the biggest US companies have links to the original oligopoly, such as AT&T, Sprint, and Verizon.

The terms of privatization have made it easy for incumbents to protect their position. To form a unified internet, the backbones must interconnect with each other and with smaller networks. This is typically how traffic travels from one corner of the internet to another. Yet because the government specified no interconnection policy when it privatized the pipes, the backbones can broker whatever deal they want. They usually let each other interconnect for free because it works to their mutual benefit, but charge smaller providers for carrying traffic. The contracts aren't just unregulated, they're generally secret. Negotiated behind closed doors with the help of nondisclosure agreements, they ensure that the deep workings of the internet are not only controlled by big corporations, but hidden from public view.

The situation with internet service providers (ISPs) is similar. These are the companies that sell consumers access to the internet rather than running its deeper networks—though in practice, they are sometimes the same companies. Market concentration in the US is intense: just four firms—Comcast, Charter, Verizon, and AT&T—account for 76 percent of all internet subscriptions in the country, and they actively collaborate to avoid competing with one another.

These behemoths have benefited not only from the terms of the settlement in 1995, but also from a series of later developments that further consolidated their position. ISPs, like backbone providers, face no obligations to do anything other than maximize their bottom line. Not only do they own the pipes and enjoy the associated profits, but they also exercise a kind of sovereign power over them. This power hinges on a simple legal definition: the question of whether companies that sell internet service should be considered "common carriers." Common carriage is an idea with a long history in the legal traditions of different countries. In the US, it descends from English common law, but the underlying elements date back to the Romans. The basic concept is that if a business is open to the general public, then it must serve everyone the same way. It must remain neutral, in other words, and not discriminate against certain users or uses of its services.

In early modern England, common carrier laws encompassed a number of trades, from bakers and brewers to surgeons and tailors. These laws enforced the principle of nondiscrimination: a ferryman had to take you across the river if he had space on his boat, and a hotelkeeper had to give you a room if she had one available. Beginning in the mid-nineteenth century, the US government, first at the state and then at the federal level, began using this framework to regulate early telecommunications networks like the telegraph. These efforts culminated in the New Deal–era Communications Act of 1934, which firmly established telecommunications providers as common carriers, subject to the oversight of the newly created Federal Communications Commission (FCC).

Sixty-two years later, the Telecommunications Act of 1996 emerged in a very different political era. FDR-style social democracy was long dead; Clintonian neoliberalism was ascendant. Industry held immense influence over the legislative process, and it was determined to use that influence to destroy any impediment to squeezing as much profit as possible from the newly privatized internet. Toward that end, the

1996 act created a distinction between providers of "telecommunications services" and "information services." The former would be subject to common carrier regulations; the latter would not. Here was the mechanism through which the next phase in the privatization of the internet would be achieved.

This phase would take longer, in part due to the particular technology that most people used to get online initially: dial-up modems. Because those modems ran over phone lines, and because those phone lines were owned and operated by companies that were still considered providers of telecommunications services, common carrier regulations still applied. Telephone companies could sell internet service over their own lines, but they also had to let other ISPs use their lines for the same purpose. The nondiscrimination principle meant they couldn't discriminate against certain users of their infrastructure, even if those users were selling internet service that competed with their own.

Gradually, however, the big ISPs would succeed in casting off these constraints. The first step came in 2002, when a Republican-led FCC under President Bush settled a long-running debate over the regulatory status of cable internet by classifying it as an information service, thus exempting it from common carrier rules. Three years later, the agency did the same for internet service sold over telephone lines. In 2015, a Democrat-led FCC under President Obama moved sharply in the other direction, designating broadband—a capacious category that refers to high-speed internet transmitted across a number of different technologies—as a common carrier telecommunications service. But in 2017, with a new agency chief installed by President Trump, the FCC reversed itself, reclassifying broadband as a lightly regulated information service. The industry crusade was complete.

The victory may prove fleeting. President Biden has signaled a desire to take a harder line, encouraging the FCC to restore the Obama-era broadband rules, though at the time of writing those rules had not yet been adopted. Even if they are, much damage has already been done, damage that will take considerable political will to undo. In particular, the unraveling of common carrier regulation that began in the early 2000s led to a major consolidation of the ISP market. In 1998, 92 percent of Americans had the choice of seven or more ISPs simply by using a modem over their phone line. But in the aftermath of a 2005 Supreme Court decision that affirmed the Bush-era deregulations, the big ISPs began refusing their competitors access to their infrastructure. If small ISPs weren't allowed to use the lines of big ISPs, they were finished: they couldn't possibly afford to build their own. Most went out of business.

Cutting big ISPs loose from common carrier rules didn't just let them kill their competition. It also enabled them to manipulate the flow of data through their pipes to their advantage. During the FCC's regulatory push under Obama, when the agency had classified broadband providers as common carriers, it enforced the principle of "net neutrality": the axiom that ISPs should treat all kinds of data the same way. When net neutrality was ended under Trump, companies like Comcast became free to ferry data across their networks however they liked. They could block access to certain sites, throttle customer speeds, and cut "paid prioritization" deals with content providers to create "fast lanes" for certain kinds of traffic.

These deals are well suited to a system where content comes from fewer sources. After all, the pipes aren't the only part of the internet held by relatively few hands; a comparable concentration of power prevails in who owns and organizes the information that passes through them. Today, six companies—Google, Netflix, Facebook, Microsoft, Apple, and Amazon—account for nearly half of all traffic on the internet. These giants have teamed up with their broadband counterparts to build shortcuts to each other's networks. Content providers like Netflix funnel data directly to broadband providers like Comcast and place caches deep within their networks, avoiding a circuitous route through the bowels of the internet.

Finding a more direct path for one's packets is something of a theme in the modern internet, in fact. Content delivery networks (CDNs) put copies of websites and other media on servers that are geographically closer to users, in order to reduce wait times. Meanwhile, small to medium-sized networks interconnect directly so they don't have to pay larger providers for transporting their data. Still, backbones remain essential for certain kinds of traffic, namely the long-haul, international kind. So the bigger content providers have decided to acquire backbones of their own. While the barrier to entry into the broadband market remains forbiddingly high—even Google was forced to abandon its ambition to have a nationwide ISP with Google Fiber—tech companies are pushing aggressively into the backbone market. In particular, they are investing in the fiber-optic submarine cables that line the floors of the world's oceans and form the internet's global arteries.

Content providers like Google, Facebook, Amazon, and Microsoft now own or lease more than half of undersea bandwidth. While these companies generally buy a share of a cable as part of a consortium, Google has been building its own infrastructure. Unlike telecoms, tech firms are not acquiring backbones in order to sell capacity, but to use them for themselves. As they continue to remake the global architecture of the internet, constructing vertically integrated digital empires that control both the pipes and the information inside them, they are remaking the internet remade by the 1990s into an even more privatized form.

The Internet's Slumlords

The proponents of a privatized internet claimed it would be good for everyone. It would lead to better service, wider access, more investment. "Innovation, expanded services, broader participation, and lower prices will arise in a market-driven arena, not in an environment that operates as a regulated industry," stated the Clinton administration's 1997 "Framework for Global Electronic Commerce." In other words, if industry were given more power over the pipes, it would use that power to build a better internet.

How well does this claim hold up? The evidence is not encouraging. After decades of deepening private control, Americans pay some of the most expensive rates in the world in exchange for awful service. Average monthly internet costs are higher in the US than in Europe or Asia, according to a 2020 study conducted by researchers at the think tank New America, while the US ranks twelfth in average connection speeds, below Romania and Thailand. Not coincidentally, American ISPs regularly sit near the bottom of the annual American Customer Satisfaction Index, even lower than airlines and health insurers.

The reason for the pitiful state of US broadband is that the high fees extracted from users aren't being reinvested to build better infrastructure, but to enrich executives and investors. Comcast's CEO earned $36.3 million in 2019, and the company, along with the other members of the broadband cartel, has spent billions of dollars on dividends and stock buybacks in order to line the pockets of its shareholders. The big ISPs are essentially slumlords. Their principal function is to fleece their customers and funnel the money upward. They charge exorbitant prices for the privilege of using their deteriorating infrastructure because people have no alternative.

Worse than exploitation, however, is exclusion: better to be gouged by a slumlord than to be homeless. And when it comes to broadband, exclusion is the reality for tens of millions of Americans. Those who suffer most from a profit-driven system belong to communities that are too poor or too remote to merit the attention of the broadband monopolists. They are ignored because more money can be made elsewhere.

The result is large disparities in access. In 2018, Microsoft researchers found that 162.8 million Americans do not use the internet at broadband speeds—almost half the country. The disconnected are disproportionately rural and low-income. About a third of rural Americans and almost half of those with household annual incomes below $30,000 lack broadband at home, especially Black and Latino households. Even those residents of low-income areas who have the option to buy home broadband service and can afford to do so often endure slow speeds owing to systematic neglect and disinvestment by ISPs, a practice known as "digital redlining."

Home broadband is not the only way people get online. The growing ubiquity of smartphones presents another path to the internet. In fact, for some 17 percent of US adults, smart-phones are their *only* path to the internet. But while smartphone-based access is better than none at all, it has serious limitations. For one, mobile providers often impose data caps that sharply limit usage. More fundamentally, the small screen and the lack of a dedicated keyboard make smartphones unsuit-able for many online activities. In 2015, when the Pew Research Center surveyed Americans who had used smartphones to apply for jobs—perhaps the most essential online activity of all—they struggled with a number of tasks, from navigating websites not optimized for mobile to entering large amounts of text and submitting required files. Smartphones simply make poor substitutes for home broadband; those who are compelled to rely on them are at a significant disadvantage.

The COVID-19 crisis greatly magnified those disadvan-tages. As lockdowns and social distancing pushed more of people's lives online, a decent home internet connection became all the more essential. In response, the many millions of Americans without one flocked to the parking lots of schools, libraries, and other institutions that continued to offer free Wi-Fi. There, they sat in their cars for hours, work-ing from "home," attending online classes, applying for unemployment, chatting with friends and loved ones.

But not everyone could make it to the parking lot. Indeed, some school districts weren't able to shift classes online during the pandemic because too many students didn't have decent internet service. There are many such students: in 2018, the Pew Research Center found that almost one in five US teen-agers had trouble completing homework assignments because they did not have reliable access to a computer or an internet connection.

"I hope that there is a lesson learned from this," Gina Millsap, the chief executive of the Topeka & Shawnee County Public Library, told the *New York Times*. "Broadband is like water and electricity now, and yet it's still being treated like a luxury." As the pandemic powerfully illustrated, a good internet connection is a necessity. It is a prerequisite for full participation in social, economic, political, and cultural life, and one that many millions of Americans don't possess.

The Possibility of Democracy

The present order of things is not merely unfair. It is fundamentally undemocratic. What is at stake is nothing less than the possibility of democracy—a possibility that an internet organized by the profit motive precludes.

Democracy is a form of life in which people rule themselves. The word comes from the Greek *demokratia*, which translates to "rule of the people"—not rule by a portion of the people, such as the rich (plutocracy) or the priests (theocracy), but by all of the people. For the people to rule, however, each person must also rule themselves. In the words of theorist Wendy Brown, democracy "is the name of a political form in which the whole of the people rule the polity and hence themselves." Self-rule at a collective level implies and involves self-rule at an individual level.

The philosopher John Dewey once observed that individual self-rule has two ingredients. The first is freedom from external coercion or constraint—from "subjection to the will and control of others." But this kind of freedom—"negative" freedom—is insufficient by itself. For people to rule themselves, they also need "positive" freedom: the freedom to set and pursue ends. And positive freedom requires *stuff*, or what Dewey calls the "resources necessary to carry purposes into effect."

Freedom isn't free, in other words. It has certain material preconditions. If you're hungry or homeless or sick—or if you're shivering in a parking lot using free Wi-Fi to attend school online because you don't have internet at home—it's hard to lead a self-determined life. Securing those material preconditions isn't simply a matter of personal will. It has to do with social choices about how resources like food and housing and health care are distributed. For people to get the things they need to be free, they must be able to participate in these choices. Thus the act of individual self-rule is always premised on the presence of collective self-rule. The power to make meaningful decisions about the course of one's own life rests on the power to contribute meaningfully to the decisions that shape everyone's lives.

This power must be rooted in something more robust than the opportunity to choose one's government representatives every few years. Elections are the minimum of democracy's meaning. Democracy requires a richer set of practices and a wider sphere of control to be fully democratic. It must, as the theorist Stuart Hall writes, take place not just occasionally and within certain circumscribed zones but "across all the centres of social activity—in private as well as public life, in personal associations as well as in compulsory obligations, in the family and the neighbourhood and the nursery and the shopping centre as well as in the public office or at the point of production." And, we might add, in the realm of the internet.

Access to the internet is one of freedom's material preconditions. It is one of the resources that people need in order to rule themselves. A system that allocates this resource solely according to the logic of profit is incapable of providing it to everyone as a matter of right. If profit is the principle that determines how connectivity is distributed, millions will be forced to go without it—those who can't afford to pay, or those who live in places that aren't profitable enough to invest in. Many more will have only a precarious grasp on it, contingent on the size and regularity of their paychecks. Even the lucky ones, those who can consistently afford the extortionate fees of the broadband cartel, will endure the abysmal speeds caused by chronic underinvestment.

Such an arrangement is undemocratic. People can't lead self-determined lives, as their access to what Dewey calls the "resources necessary to carry purposes into effect" is nonexistent, limited, or fragile. Market dependence makes freedom's material foundations precarious. Markets don't give you what you need—they give you what you can afford. And what you can afford depends on how and whether you can earn a wage.

Individual self-rule isn't possible under these restraints, at least not on a wide scale. Neither is collective self-rule, since the decisions that affect people's lives—in this case, those that pertain to the organization of the internet—are made without those people's input. Such decisions are left in the hands of the executives and investors of private firms, who in turn must operate within the parameters set by the profit motive. Capitalism is a perpetual motion machine, driven by continuous accumulation. Profit powers this machine. Without it, accumulation comes to a halt, and firms go bankrupt.

The pursuit of profit isn't a choice, then. It's a necessity. One of the strangest things about capitalism is the fact that the people who control the perpetual motion machine—the capitalists—do not really control it. They are like characters in a play. They have a role to perform. Different actors can perform a role differently, but the script remains more or less the same. Accumulation must continue, which means that profit must always be the primary consideration.

This makes capitalists a peculiar kind of ruling class. They rule, but not completely, since they are in turn ruled by a higher power—"an inhuman power [that] rules over everything," to borrow a phrase from the young Karl Marx. It is inhuman because it is not the rule of a person but of an imperative: the imperative to accumulate. This decree is absolute. No capitalist, no matter how powerful, can disobey it. If they do, they cease to be a capitalist: accumulation halts, and the competition puts them out of business.

Understanding this basic law helps clarify how power functions in a profit-driven internet. The individuals who control the companies that control the internet do not really control the internet. Their choices matter, but their range of possible choices is constrained. They must choose to feed the engine of accumulation, in one way or another. This restricted choice in turn restricts the choices of others: in an internet organized by the profit motive, not everyone can obtain the resources they need to freely choose the course of their own lives. Nor can everyone participate in the decisions that affect them. This isn't just because most people aren't executives and investors. At a deeper level, even the decisions of the decision-makers are delimited by an imperative that nobody controls. The people can't rule because, in a sense, nobody can.

Yet the desire for self-determination is hard to kill. It finds a way to persist, even under hostile conditions. The pipes of the internet have been privatized so thoroughly over the past two and a half decades that it can be hard to imagine what an alternative might look like. Fortunately, there are communities actively engaged in constructing such an alternative. They are experimenting with different models for owning and organizing networks. They are finding ways to weaken the programming of the profit motive and to strengthen the conditions for democratic control. They are discovering the embryonic forms of an internet where the people rule.

3

The People's Pipes

In 1935, the residents of Chattanooga, Tennessee, were living in one of the poorest parts of the country in the middle of the Great Depression. Among the many things in distressingly short supply was electricity. Power, long available in the big cities, remained scarce in rural areas like the Tennessee Valley. This wasn't an accident. Rather, it reflected a basic business logic. Private monopolies dominated the electricity market. This "power trust" was notorious for refusing to serve communities it didn't consider profitable, and for price-gouging the ones it did.

So Chattanoogans decided to take their power supply out of private hands. They voted overwhelmingly for a municipal bond issue that funded the creation of a city-owned electricity distribution system called the Electric Power Board. The utility itself wasn't the only part that was public; so was the current that coursed through it. The Electric Power Board would distribute electricity generated by the new Tennessee Valley Authority (TVA), a federal corporation created by the Roosevelt administration to electrify the region.

Seventy-five years later, Chattanooga embarked on another experiment in public provision. In 2010, the Electric Power Board, now rebranded EPB, began offering broadband service. More specifically, it began offering the fastest broadband service in the country: 1 gigabit per second, more than two hundred times faster than the national average at the time. These speeds gave the network its nickname: "the Gig."

The story of the Gig began two years earlier, when EPB—which remains one of the largest publicly owned electric distribution utilities in the country—began building a "smart grid." Funded by a bond issue and a federal stimulus grant, this undertaking promised to make the grid more efficient by embedding sensors and other digital devices that monitored the system in real time. Problems could be detected early, which would help reduce outages and improve reliability.

The smart grid didn't just end up saving EPB money. It also handed them the infrastructure they needed to become an ISP. The smart grid ran on a fiber-optic network, which is what enabled the monitoring devices to communicate. The same network could be repurposed to offer internet service as well. The speeds were fast because fiber already ran all the way to people's homes—an architecture known, unsurprisingly, as "fiber to the home." Rather than limping along a creaky telephone line or a coaxial cable across the "last mile" between Chattanoogans and their ISP, data could travel at the speed of light. The same technology used to shuttle packets from one continent to another through the backbones of the internet was now handling traffic along Chattanooga's last mile.

In the years since, the Gig has become the most famous municipal broadband network in the country. It has also become one of the country's most popular ISPs, by charging reasonable rates for some of the fastest residential speeds in the world. Moreover, it makes access a priority: low-income families are eligible for a special plan that gives them 100 megabit-per-second service for less than half the standard rate. EPB had hoped to offer it for even less, but a state law prohibits utilities from selling services below cost to prevent them from undercutting private firms.

While the Gig is especially well known, it is far from unique. The Institute for Local Self-Reliance estimates that more than nine hundred communities across the United States are served by publicly or cooperatively owned networks. Most are under municipal ownership, like the Gig. Many others are operated by rural electric and telephone cooperatives that trace their origins to the New Deal, when the Roosevelt administration seeded them with federal loans as part of the same rural electrification campaign that saw the creation of the TVA. Such cooperatives are owned and controlled by their members, who are also the users of their services.

Publicly and cooperatively owned "community networks" do things that private ISPs can't. First, they can supply better service at lower cost. A group of Harvard researchers found that "community-owned fiber-to-the-home (FTTH) networks in the United States generally charge less for entry-level broadband service" than private providers. This is because, unlike their corporate counterparts, they don't exist to enrich investors. But their affordable rates also reflect a deeper fact: that community networks are guided by a different philosophy. "Community-owned ISPs typically regard the provision of high-speed Internet access as an end in itself and a means to achieving other community benefits," observed the

Harvard researchers. In other words, they tend to focus on social needs, such as universal connectivity, rather than profit maximization.

This makes them uniquely effective in places where profits are hard to maximize. Rural North Dakota is one such place. You might expect the best internet service in the state to be found in the cities, such as Fargo. Instead, it's in the farmlands of Nelson County (population 2,879), Logan County (population 1,850), and Kidder County (population 2,480), where 100 percent of residents can get gigabit speeds. A report from the Institute for Local Self-Reliance found that rural North Dakotans are not only more likely to have access to fiber to the home than urban North Dakotans, but also, remarkably, they are more likely to have access to fiber to the home than urban Americans in general.

The backstory began in the 1990s, when a coalition of North Dakota telephone cooperatives teamed up with a handful of small telephone companies to purchase more than sixty rural exchanges from a major telecom. This infrastructure became the foundation for a statewide fiber network, which the cooperatives then wired into their communities with the help of federal subsidies. Rural North Dakota, like rural regions everywhere, has long been neglected by the broadband giants for being insufficiently remunerative. Yet this hasn't prevented big ISPs from collecting ample amounts of money from the FCC in exchange for promises to expand rural access. These promises are rarely kept: the companies take the cash and refuse to invest. Cooperatives, on the other hand, can make a little public support go a long way. "Our goal isn't to put money back into shareholders' pockets," explained Robin Anderson, a veteran of North Dakota's cooperative scene. "Our goal is to provide the best service possible and keep reinvesting in that network."

The People Rule

Community networks offer a model for what it might look like to reorganize the pipes of the internet around human need. Still, they must operate within certain constraints. Just because these entities are publicly or cooperatively owned does not exempt them from market imperatives. They must compete, sell a commodity, and earn revenue to survive. Yet the fact that they are owned and organized differently than private firms enables them to deviate—sometimes slightly, sometimes significantly—from the logic of accumulation.

Crucially, this is not just a matter of mission statements. It is rooted in legal mechanisms that compel community networks to function differently than private ones. For instance, most rural cooperatives, like those in North Dakota, are granted a federal tax exemption as 501(c)(12) organizations. To retain this exemption, they must operate at cost and return any excess revenue to their members. They can cover the expenses incurred by providing service, but they can't pile up profits. They must also guarantee democratic control of the cooperative by holding regular elections for the board.

Few community networks are as democratic as they could be. At their best, however, they empower their users to determine how they are run. And this is ultimately what distinguishes community networks from their corporate rivals: it's not solely the fact of public or cooperative ownership, but the forms of collective governance and popular participation that these alternative ownership models make possible. To put people over profit, you need to create spaces where the people can rule.

A particularly powerful illustration of this principle comes from Detroit, one of the worst-connected cities in the country. The appalling condition of broadband in Detroit is a testament to how inequalities in connectivity tend to be highly racialized: in a city that is almost 80 percent Black, upward of 60 percent of low-income households have no home broadband. A staggering 70 percent of school-age children have no home internet of any kind.

Since 2016, organizers with the Equitable Internet Initiative (EII) have been working to end this crisis. A program of the Detroit Community Technology Project (DCTP), EII uses money raised from foundations and a donated upstream connection to bring broadband to hundreds of homes in Detroit. A system of wireless transmitters beams an internet signal to partnering community groups in three different neighborhoods, and from there to people's homes. These homes not only receive internet for zero or low cost, depending on residents' ability to pay, they also get access to a private network—an intranet—that lets them communicate with one another and find information on local resources like food pantries and translation services. During the COVID-19 pandemic, as connectivity became even more crucial, EII organizers also helped create several Wi-Fi hotspots in the three neighborhoods.

"If the community has ownership of the infrastructure, then they're more likely to participate in its maintenance, evolution, and innovation," Diana Nucera, founder and former director of DCTP, told *YES!* magazine. This participation is quite direct, as the people responsible for building and maintaining the network are residents of the neighborhoods themselves, trained by DCTP and its partner organizations to serve as "digital stewards." Digital stewards do everything from installing wireless dishes and configuring routers to explaining how different technologies work and how to use them, especially to elderly neighbors who have little experience with the internet.

But digital stewards aren't just technicians. They are also trained to be community organizers. They receive both a technical and a political education, with a curriculum that draws on the work of revolutionary thinkers like Paulo Freire and Grace Lee Boggs. This points to the deeper purpose of the project, which is to increase not just the connectivity of Detroit's poorer neighborhoods, but their *connectedness*. "We are working towards a future where neighbors are authentically connected," read the Working Principles of the Equitable Internet Initiative, "with relationships of mutual aid that sustain the social, economic, and environmental health of neighborhoods."

Such an approach is a far cry from technocratic strategies to close the "digital divide" that aim merely at expanding access—and, further, imagine that doing so will solve poverty, a fantasy that scholar Daniel Greene calls "the access doctrine." Connectivity is essential, but so is transforming how people connect. Simply plugging more users into a privatized internet does nothing to change how the internet is owned or organized, much less how it is experienced. The organizers in Detroit are finding another way to connect. In the process, they are challenging privatization in two senses. A community-owned network that gives users cheap or free service is a very different model for organizing the pipes of the internet than the one that has prevailed since 1995. It upends the assumption, long dominant in policymaking circles, that the internet should be controlled by private firms and run for the purpose of profit maximization. Thanks to EII, Detroiters who would otherwise be too poor to afford internet service can look up bus schedules and video-chat with their grandchildren. They have access to a resource they need in order to exercise meaningful control of their lives.

But by embedding the network within a community organizing effort, EII is also subverting privatization in a subtler sense. The particular way of owning and operating the internet that triumphed in the 1990s has also encouraged a particular way of experiencing the internet: privately. Privatization does not just describe the political process whereby the internet became a business, but a social process whereby people's mode of interacting with the internet was engineered for business's benefit. Passive and isolated consumers are the profitable end point of this process: a collection of atomized individuals, alone with our glowing screens.

The organizers in Detroit are proposing another possibility. They are building a network that brings people into new relationships of trust and support and mutual concern, forged in the course of caring for collective infrastructure and caring for one another. The users of this network are neither passive nor isolated. They are active participants in the growth, maintenance, and governance of their infrastructure, and members of a collectivity. The relationships that compose this collectivity, the organizers of EII believe, can serve as the basis for a movement of social transformation. They can form the sinews of the organizing muscle needed to deliver real self-determination for the poor and working-class residents of Detroit. Self-determination in the digital sphere, and the solidarities it generates, offers a point of departure for achieving self-determination in all fields of social life.

Making an Example

By serving excluded communities, by offering more affordable and more accessible service, and by enabling a degree of community control over their operations, public and cooperatively owned networks in places like Chattanooga and North Dakota and Detroit are living critiques of the market-first model. Perhaps this is why corporate ISPs have spent so much money trying to destroy them. In one state after another, telecoms have lobbied legislators to pass laws that prevent communities from creating their own networks. Thanks to their efforts, municipal broadband is restricted or banned outright in eighteen states. Another favored tactic is lawsuits, which tie up community ventures in the courts and force them to rack up expensive legal fees. This is exactly how Comcast tried (and failed) to derail Chattanooga's Gig.

The intensity with which the broadband giants prosecute their crusade against community networks might seem a little excessive. After all, these are publicly traded companies with market valuations in the hundreds of billions of dollars. Their opponents are tiny by comparison, and pose no meaningful threat to their market share. But these firms have the wisdom to recognize that such a threat may very well materialize if people come to see community networks as a feasible alternative to the corporate model. "What the broadband cartel fears," explain the scholars Victor Pickard and David Elliot

Berman, "is less the near term loss of market share than the long-term threat of a good example." The demonstration effect is the real danger. A popular and well-functioning community network might help make credible a hypothesis that decades of privatizers have worked hard to deny: that there is an alternative way to arrange the pipes of the internet.

Neoliberalism is, among other things, an enforced closure of the political imagination. Among its rallying cries is the slogan made famous by Margaret Thatcher, "there is no alternative." This statement masquerades as a simple description of reality, but the reality it describes must be made true by deliberately foreclosing such alternatives. Neoliberal politicians are good at producing evidence for their beliefs when in power; for example, by defunding and undermining particular functions of government and then pointing to the subsequent failures to claim that government can't possibly perform such functions.

The privatization of the internet's pipes in the 1990s took place within just such a political context. Alternatives to privatization existed, but they were never seriously entertained. The depth of the consensus around maximum marketization—a consensus that companies poised to profit from privatization helped consolidate—lent an air of inevitability to the proceedings. A highly contingent outcome became, through the alchemy of ideology, a necessary and natural one.

Community networks give us an opportunity to revisit, and to reverse, this history. They represent the rudiments of a real alternative. This alternative is being constructed in the cracks and edges of our corporatized system, as communities find creative ways to meet their needs. A democratic internet is not an ideal to which reality must reconcile itself, but something that is already being worked out in practice. It is not a schematic to be implemented from above, but a set of experiments emerging from below. These experiments are necessarily limited, however: if there is any hope of their cohering into a radically new arrangement, they must be defended, extended, and deepened.

Defend and Extend

Defending community networks begins with defeating the laws that telecoms have engineered to sabotage them. In 2015, a Democrat-led FCC took a step in this direction by preempting statutes in North Carolina and Tennessee that prohibit municipal broadband utilities from expanding their service areas. But a federal appeals court blocked the move, claiming the agency didn't have the authority. Dismantling the obstructions of the broadband cartel will ultimately require an act of Congress.

Merely removing roadblocks will hardly level the playing field, however. Even if they were no longer hamstrung by hostile state legislatures, community networks would still be going up against large firms with extensive resources at their disposal. Playing defense is not enough. Networks will not only need to be defended but extended.

Both Bernie Sanders and Elizabeth Warren put forward plans for doing so during the 2020 Democratic Party presidential primaries. Warren proposed giving $85 billion in federal grants to cooperatives, local governments, nonprofits, and tribes to build infrastructure for "high-speed public broadband." Sanders called for $150 billion in both grants and technical assistance to municipalities and states "to build publicly owned and democratically controlled, co-operative, or open access broadband networks." Significantly, Sanders also tied his proposal to the Green New Deal. The same networks that deliver internet service could support smart grids that improve energy efficiency, as in Chattanooga.

This kind of support is indispensable for bringing community networks from the margins to the mainstream. It could help modernize existing networks, and create thousands of new ones. Where possible, new networks should be planted in existing institutions that already have technical expertise, infrastructure, or relationships with the community; an electric and telephone cooperative that has thousands of member-owners will probably make a better community network than one made from scratch, for instance.

Municipal governments also have a lot of potential in this regard. Many have already built networks for internal use to lower their telecommunications costs. Washington, DC, has a municipally owned fiber network that serves local government agencies, as well as hundreds of community nonprofits such as health care clinics, homeless shelters, and counseling centers at reduced rates. The city also sells the use of its network to last-mile ISP providers that want to bring internet service to households, particularly those in the city's least-connected areas. There's no reason the network couldn't extend into the last mile itself and serve Washington's neighborhoods—except for the fact that the city has signed franchise agreements with corporate ISPs like Verizon and Comcast that prohibit it from doing so.

Even where there is a foundation to build on, however, public subsidies will be needed. But these subsidies shouldn't come for free. Rather, they should be made conditional on recipients embracing certain practices and priorities, with an eye toward developing what makes community networks distinctive: their democratic aspect.

Along these lines, both the Sanders and Warren plans stipulate that any network receiving public support meet certain minimum speed and affordability requirements. Yet this approach can be taken further, to the point of actually reorganizing how networks are run. Researchers Thomas M. Hanna, Mathew Lawrence, Adrienne Buller, and Miriam Brett propose requiring grant recipients to "embrace democratic and participatory values and governance." This might mean having networks create a governing council of immediately recallable delegates, elected by the community, or even to implement participatory governance programs that enable community members to directly determine how resources are allocated.

A further advantage of public funding is that it can lower costs for users. This is crucial, given how many people don't have decent internet because they can't afford it. According to the Pew Research Center, half of those who have no home broadband say it'sW because the monthly fee is too high. Community networks can help by making access more affordable—but they generally don't make access free.

What if they did offer free service? Hanna, Lawrence, Buller, and Brett recommend using public money for this purpose. Not only would the one-time costs of laying the fiber for community networks be covered, but also the ongoing costs of their operation—yet only on the condition that they "move towards providing service for free, or at highly reduced rates."

Making this more feasible is the fact that fiber infrastructure, once built, doesn't cost much to run. This is because fiber is more reliable and resilient than copper or coaxial cables, and so requires less maintenance; it also uses less energy. Fiber is actually the cheapest kind of network to operate: a 2020 study by the Fiber Broadband Association found that the annual operating expenses of an FTTH network were about half those of a cable internet network on a per-home basis. The public sector could cover these expenses through its support of community networks. An internet connection would cease to be a commodity and become a social good, provided to all as a matter of right.

Wiring an Ecosystem

Community networks already exhibit a tendency to place people over profit. But this tendency, in order to become something more than a tendency, must be cultivated and consolidated through public policy. If that happens, local experiments in public and cooperative ownership can become the seeds from which a very different internet can grow: a deprivatized internet where everyone has access to the resources they need to lead self-determined lives and an opportunity to participate in the decisions that affect them.

Throwing money at community networks, with strings attached, isn't the only way to apply the power of the public sector. Another useful tool is procurement. Procurement is the process whereby government agencies buy what they need to perform their functions. One of the things they need is an internet connection. So why not have them purchase that connection from a community network, rather than from a corporate ISP like Comcast? This would be no small achievement. Nearly 20 million people work for state and local governments across the country; in many cities, the public sector is the largest employer.

Hospitals and universities also tend to loom large in local economies. A 2021 study found that they were the top employers in twenty-seven states. Sometimes these entities are public, sometimes private, but they all benefit from public money and tax breaks. What if, in exchange, they were required to purchase their internet access from community networks? Their subscription fees could help defray the costs of supplying households with free internet from the same fiber.

These relationships wouldn't have to be limited to community networks; in fact, they could buttress an entire ecosystem of new economic organizations. This is the idea behind what thinkers Joe Guinan and Martin O'Neill call "community wealth building": a strategy for increasing "democratic collective ownership of the local economy" by tapping the procurement budgets of public and quasi-public "anchor institutions." As a model, they point to the Evergreen Cooperatives in Cleveland, a cluster of worker-owned cooperatives including a laundry, a greenhouse, and a solar energy company that count two major medical centers, a university, and the city government among their clients. Another source of inspiration is Preston, a city in the United Kingdom that has undertaken a similar, if more extensive, set of experiments.

Embedding community networks in these kinds of arrangements would both buoy them financially and reinforce the democratic values that should define them, values that push against the inhuman power of the profit motive and toward the possibility of people ruling themselves together.

The point is not to replace the broadband cartel with a bunch of community Comcasts, but with entities of an entirely different kind.

Small Is Not Always Beautiful

While community networks are crucial, we can't rely on them for everything. This is because their greatest strength—their rootedness in a particular place—is also the source of certain weaknesses.

Community networks are, as the name suggests, based in specific communities. The size of the service area can vary—some cover a neighborhood, others a county—but in general, the "community" in question is a fairly local one. This localism has several advantages. Democratic deliberation and decision-making can take place in person, and at a manageable scale. Face-to-face relationships can be forged among the people who collectively control the network, making it easier to build trust. Local circumstances can be taken into account, such as those presented by the unique features of the natural or built environment.

Not all community networks can or should look like traditional ISPs: different network topologies or technologies may be better suited to a community's requirements. Some may want to optimize for resiliency with mesh networking, for example, which uses direct connections between nodes to minimize single points of failure. This is particularly useful for disaster scenarios, because so long as any nodes remain, they can continue to communicate. When Hurricane Sandy flooded the Brooklyn neighborhood of Red Hook in 2012, the power went out and cell phones stopped working, but the area's mesh network stayed up, keeping residents connected and enabling them to coordinate the emergency response.

If localism brings many benefits, however, it also carries some significant risks. The community is not something to fetishize. "Local control" has a long, racist history in American life. Under its banner, communities have resisted school desegregation, blocked affordable housing projects, and hoarded public money in the places that least need it. There are rich communities and poor communities, and the former tend to find ways of keeping their advantages out of the hands of the latter. Decentralization is not inherently democratizing: it can just as easily serve to concentrate power as to distribute it.

Ideally, we could come up with a synthesis, one that allows us to retain the special strengths of the local while mitigating its various risks through regional and national interventions. This would be a delicate balancing act, a matter of avoiding exclusionary fragmentation at one extreme and top-down technocracy on the other. While this approach is motivated by political concerns—the need to ensure that everyone has a high-quality connection, no matter their zip code—there are also technical considerations. We can't transform the internet purely at the local level. This is because the internet is neither local nor national nor global but a complex combination of all three. It operates at a number of different scales, and so must any project to transform it.

You might think of these different scales in terms of size—neighborhood, city, region, world—but it also makes sense to think of them in terms of depth. Imagine you're standing on the surface of a planet. If you want to go somewhere close by, you can walk along the surface to get there. But if you want to go somewhere far away—say, to the other side of the planet—it might make more sense to dig a tunnel through the center. Similarly, the further your data travels across the internet, the deeper the networks it will have to traverse. If a computer in Chattanooga wants to talk to a server in Lagos, its packets will pass through the center of the system.

The center of the system is a strange place. The writer Andrew Blum calls it "the interim internet": an in-between zone, populated by relatively few humans and a lot of expensive machinery. To reach this zone, community networks must pay to interconnect with larger providers at facilities called internet exchange points. Here, racks of routers and a handful of technicians orchestrate the complex flight of data around the country and around the world, linking the last mile with the first, the tributaries with the backbones, all inside nondescript buildings protected by several layers of security.

This is where the stitching together of the many scales of the internet occurs, and its handiwork has considerable downstream consequences. Whose traffic will receive priority? Which regions will be best served? As long as private firms control the core networks, these questions will continue to be answered by executives and investors, and always with an eye toward profit. Democratizing the internet must involve turning even its deepest corridors into places where people, and not profit, rule.

In fact, this may become a practical necessity. If community networks began to displace corporate ISPs, the broadband cartel might use its power to block their upstream path. Of the four firms that account for 76 percent of all internet subscriptions in the US, three also operate backbones. They could refuse to work with community networks, leaving them stranded. This is the legacy of privatization: a corporate dictatorship over critical infrastructure. Creating alternatives may be the only hope for community networks to achieve their full potential.

The Green New Deal might offer one possibility for doing so. Climate activists have been calling for a national electricity grid that could efficiently distribute renewable energy across the US. "When clouds soften the California sun, wind from Texas can charge Los Angeles's buses; when the Georgia sun sets, offshore winds on the eastern seaboard could power Atlanta's streetlights," write Kate Aronoff, Alyssa Battistoni, Daniel Aldana Cohen, and Thea Riofrancos in their co-authored book *A Planet to Win*. Such a grid could be made "smart" by laying fiber along it, which could in turn provide the foundation for a new deprivatized backbone serving community networks nationwide. The backbone could be managed by a federal agency, or perhaps by a federation of cooperatives, each responsible for different aspects or branches of the network. If needed, its footprint could be enlarged further by acquiring the thousands of miles of unused "dark" fiber buried across the country, and extended overseas by taking a stake in a submarine cable.

This may seem impractical, even utopian. It's one thing to defend and extend community networks, quite another to storm the fortresses lying upstream. But if the effort to deprivatize the pipes of the internet remains confined to one segment, it won't survive. Its enemies will use its isolation to undermine it, wielding their control of the internet's core to crush democratic experimentation at the edges. "Whoever finishes a revolution only halfway digs his own grave," says

Robespierre in Georg Büchner's play *Danton's Death*. A revolution must always keep moving. Otherwise, its victories will be small and partial, and easily reversed.

4

From Below

From the edges to the core, from the neighborhoods to the backbones, making a democratic internet must be the work of a movement. This is what was missing in the 1990s, and its absence enabled industry to push through privatization of a particularly comprehensive kind. It wasn't a failure of ideas—activists had ideas—but of power. Other possibilities existed, such as a "public lane on the information superhighway," but the instrument for making those possibilities practical did not: namely, masses of people willing to take disruptive action to overcome the opposition of industry and its faithful representatives in government.

Before such action can occur, however, a lot of talking must take place. Movements are made through organizing, and organizing consists mostly of conversations. Conversations about the problems in people's lives and where those problems come from, and what would be needed to solve them. Organizers listen, make the case, and address the concerns that arise.

When it comes to deprivatizing the pipes of the internet, three concerns in particular are likely to arise. The first is the potential cost of such a venture. How will we pay for it?

To begin with, it's worth pointing out that we already pay heavily for the present arrangement: the broadband cartel regularly receives large infusions of public cash. Incredibly, the stated rationale for these infusions is to help expand access. In other words, the preferred strategy among policymakers for solving the connectivity crisis is to give immense sums of public money to the firms that are responsible for causing it. In the words of one Detroit Community Technology Project staffer, "We're trying to close the digital divide by paying Comcast and AT&T, who are responsible for the digital divide."

There are a number of federal programs, and various initiatives at the state and local levels, that provide corporate ISPs with billions of dollars' worth of subsidies, tax breaks, and other incentives in the hopes of boosting broadband investment. Take the FCC's Universal Service Fund. This fund is financed by a tax on telecommunications providers, which in practice amounts to a tax on consumers since it generally shows up as a surcharge in Americans' phone bills. The money is then distributed to ISPs in the form of loans and grants, which are supposed to help them do things like expand rural broadband.

The problem with this approach is that ISPs typically pocket the cash and fail to deliver. Handing public money to private firms tends to enrich the firms while yielding little in the way of public benefit. To cite one example of many, a major ISP called CenturyLink began receiving $505.7 million in annual support from the Universal Service Fund to pay for broadband deployment in underserved areas in 2015. Five years later, the company told the FCC it had only met the mandated milestones in ten states out of thirty-three—fewer than a third. During these years, CenturyLink's CEO was one of the highest-paid executives in the industry, earning $35.7 million in 2018.

The amount of money involved is considerable. According to policy analyst Daniel Hanley, the FCC and the US Department of Agriculture gave more than $22 billion to corporate ISPs to help improve rural connectivity over just a four-year period, from 2013 to 2017. And in January 2020, the FCC promised another $20 billion over the next ten years for the same purpose. Yet, as Hanley observes, "the mechanism of feeding private companies giant sums of money for broadband build-out simply hasn't worked." Indeed, the mechanism's failure to work may be precisely the point: so long as millions of people remain un- or under-connected, the public money can continue to flow. The slumlords of the internet can keep getting paid for promising to fix the problems they created.

This money would be better spent on the build-out of publicly and cooperatively owned networks, and on providing ongoing operational support to ensure that such networks can offer service for free, or as close to free as possible. Still, other sources of revenue will be required. One idea would be to revive the differential fee structure proposed by the advocates of a "public lane" for the internet in the 1990s. Businesses would pay more for access, particularly businesses over a certain size; individuals would pay less, or nothing at all. Another approach would be to target large tech companies like Google and Facebook with a digital services tax on revenues from online advertising. This is an especially deep well to draw from: the combined revenue of Google and Facebook alone came to more than $230 billion in 2019, the majority from ads. The scholar David Elliot Berman proposes a third possibility: tax Comcast, Verizon, and the other members of the broadband cartel. "They are responsible for the sorry state of broadband in this country: we should make them pay to fix it," he writes.

Competition Is Overrated

Another concern may emerge here. A system of community networks that supplied service for free, or nearly free, would almost certainly put the broadband giants out of business, particularly if the latter were also taxed to help subsidize the former. Wouldn't that be anti-competitive? The answer is yes, and that's fine.

Competition is routinely presented as the solution to the country's broadband problems. Indeed, most advocates of community networks see them in these terms: as ways to put pressure on the big ISPs, thus forcing them to improve service. And it's true that creating more competitive markets for internet access would bring certain benefits. Multiple studies show that more competition leads to lower prices and higher speeds.

But competition is a crude mechanism. It can only do so much. A study conducted in 2016 by the consulting firm Analysis Group examined four years of broadband pricing data from a hundred local markets and concluded that the biggest beneficiaries of more competition were those who purchased the costlier, higher-speed plans: monthly rates for such plans fell roughly 35 percent when a market went from having one to two providers. This is only a single report, of course, but it illustrates a broader point: competition works best for customers who are worth competing for. Many people will remain "bad" customers no matter how much competition exists, because they're too poor, or they live in places too remote, to be profitable. Moreover, improving service in such communities typically requires expensive infrastructure investments that won't pay for themselves.

Fortunately, there is a way to reduce prices and increase speeds while also expanding access: using the power of the public sector to extend and deepen community networks. Such networks have the further advantage of giving their users control over how they are run—something that no amount of competition among private firms can provide. This control is crucial; among other things, it means that users can enforce standards around minimum speeds and reliability. It also means they can intervene to prevent the network from engaging in predatory practices with their data.

These practices reflect another problem that more competition won't solve. An ISP that faces competitive pressure is just as likely to spy on its customers' browser history and sell that information to advertisers, for instance, or to violate net neutrality by creating premium "fast lanes" for certain kinds of content. Indeed, competitive pressure may push firms to do these sorts of things more frequently, as they search for additional revenue to offset thinning profit margins.

Nor can we rely on ideas of expanded consumer choice, not least because it is an odd concept to apply to something like internet access. There aren't different flavors or colors or styles. Everyone wants the same thing: the fastest, most reliable connection at the lowest price. It's a simple optimization problem, in other words, and if the local community network can help people solve it, it's doubtful they will miss the experience of shopping around for a provider. Rather than a choice, access to the internet has become so essential to most people's lives that it more closely resembles housing and health care: that is, something people can't choose *not* to consume. For this reason, it makes more sense to think of the costs associated with getting online as a tax—and a regressive one at that. Why not then make the tax fairer, by shifting its burden to the companies that profit most from the internet?

To its supporters, consumer choice isn't important just for subjective reasons, but for objective ones. Consumer choice is the propulsion that sets the machinery of competition in motion. People choose to consume from one firm instead of another. In doing so, they make their preferences felt. As those aggregated preferences lead to increased revenue for the favored firm, the discipline of the market compels all firms to adjust their behavior as a result: by dropping prices, improving quality, or doing whatever else they need to do to attract consumers.

This is a descriptive account of how competitive markets work under capitalism. But it's also something else: a theory of power. It says that the best way for human beings to exercise power over the conditions of their lives is through their capacity as market actors. If they want better internet service, they can make different consumption choices. And if market conditions are sufficiently competitive, the signals that those choices transmit will eventually result in better internet service.

In reality, this is a weak way to exercise power. It consigns people to a passive role with a narrow range of action. They are, at best, semaphores whose signals can influence the production and investment decisions of firms at a distance. Such influence has severe limits: competition can lower fees and improve speeds, but many people still won't be able to afford service, or will live in places where it is not profitable to invest. Meanwhile, the firms remain accountable to their investors, not to the communities that depend on them. There is no guarantee that people will be able to obtain the resources they need to live self-determined lives; they certainly won't be able to participate in the decisions that affect them.

This is another example of neoliberalism's impoverishing effect on our political imagination. As Wendy Brown explains, neoliberalism "configures human beings exhaustively as market actors, always, only, and everywhere as *homo oeconomicus*." Yet there is another way to think about what it means to be human: *Homo politicus*. This is the human being as a political animal: what Aristotle had in mind when he wrote that man is "by nature an animal intended to live in a polis." *Homo politicus* exercises power not indirectly and individually, as an isolated stream of market signals, but directly and collectively, as the co-legislator of its social world. People argue, debate, deliberate, and decide how to govern themselves together. *Homo politicus* is what makes democracy possible.

Spy Machines

One final area of concern involves state surveillance. State surveillance is an omnipresent feature of online life and the US government runs an especially far-reaching spy machine, as revealed by Edward Snowden's disclosures in 2013. Any plan that involves leveraging the power of the public sector to transform the internet will raise fears that it could increase state surveillance, or that it could help the state engage in other kinds of repression: blocking access to websites that are considered subversive, for example, or suspending internet access entirely, as India's government does frequently, particularly in the border region of Kashmir.

But state spying, censorship, and shutdowns are all quite easy in a privatized system. The reality is that governments do what they like regardless of who owns the internet's infrastructure. The National Security Agency taps into undersea fiber-optic cables to snoop on the packets that pass through them—the fact that these cables are controlled by private firms presents no barrier. The same is true of internet shutdowns: governments in India and elsewhere routinely force private ISPs to suspend service.

Digital authoritarianism and private ownership are entirely compatible. There is no reason to believe that an internet with more municipally owned broadband networks, or even a federally owned backbone, would make authoritarians any happier than a completely privatized one. It's not a matter of whether the state has power over the pipes—it always does—but how that power is used. And there is precedent to suggest that power can be used in a positive way. In fact, we already have a good example of a publicly owned network that has long made privacy a priority: the post office.

The post office was the first communications network in the United States. From the start, it enshrined the confidentiality of messages into its everyday operations. In 1782, the Continental Congress, still at war with the British, passed an ordinance that prohibited postal workers from opening the mail; in 1792, the Congress of the now-independent United States wrote this prohibition into the statute that officially created the post office. "The ideological premise that government control over the network did not automatically give it the right to use that control for surveillance purposes was part of the American postal system from the beginning," writes the legal scholar Anuj C. Desai. According to Desai, this premise would go on to inspire the interpretation of the Fourth Amendment that forms the basis for modern privacy law.

The history of the post office is not without its blemishes. Under direction from Congress, it has also served at various times as an agent of government censorship, as when the notoriously repressive Espionage Act of 1917 gave postal officials wide latitude to block the circulation of publications deemed harmful to the war effort. Still, the enduring principle of postal privacy shows that it's possible for publicly owned networks to respect the rights of their users.

Laws and regulations are useful, but far from sufficient. The best way to guarantee that public institutions serve the people is the presence of the people themselves within those institutions. States tend to concentrate power, distributing decision-making authority upward. Democratization means making power flow in the opposite direction: downward and outward. This involves redefining how the public sector functions at all levels, by introducing what researchers Andrew Cumbers and Thomas M. Hanna call "inclusive and expansive governance structures." Such structures could place power in the hands of those with most at stake: the users of public services, community residents, and public sector workers, among others. Drawing on the state to make the internet's pipes more democratic requires making a different kind of state: one that "is rooted in, constantly draws energy from, and is pushed actively by, popular forces," in the words of Stuart Hall. Only such a state can help uproot the regime installed by privatization and put something better in its place.

This regime's reign extends much farther than the pipes, however. The process of privatization that began in the 1990s would continue up the stack, rising from the cables and routers of the internet's basement into its upper floors. And this next stage would arguably be more important, since up the stack is where more money is made and more power is held. As I write, Comcast is worth more than $260 billion; Google is worth more than $1.7 trillion. The telecoms are big, but the so-called platforms are creatures of another scale. Up the stack is also where privatization has taken a more complex, and more creative, course. Here the question was not how to make money from plugging people into the internet. It was how to make money from what they did once they logged on.

PART II

THE PLATFORMS

5

Up the Stack

On Labor Day weekend in 1995, a software engineer made a website. It wasn't his first. At twenty-eight, Pierre Omidyar had followed the standard accelerated trajectory of Silicon Valley: he had learned to code in seventh grade, and was on track to becoming a millionaire before the age of thirty by having his startup bought by Microsoft. Now he worked for a company that made software for handheld computers, widely expected to be the next big thing. But he was fascinated by the internet. So he spent his spare time online, tinkering with side projects. The idea for this particular project would be simple: a website where people could buy and sell.

Buying and selling was still a relatively new idea on the internet. The NSFNET backbone had been decommissioned only five months earlier, marking the end of the era of public ownership. The question was no longer whether the internet would be a business, but what kind of business it would be. Companies big and small were racing to come up with the answer. In May, Bill Gates circulated a memo at Microsoft announcing that the internet was the company's top priority. In July, a former investment banker named Jeff Bezos launched an online storefront called Amazon.com, which claimed to be "Earth's biggest bookstore." In August, Netscape, creator of the most popular web browser, held its initial public offering (IPO). By the end of the first day of trading, the company was worth almost $3 billion—despite being unprofitable. Wall Street was paying attention. The dot-com bubble was starting to inflate.

If the internet of 1995 inspired dreams of a lucrative future, however, the reality ran far behind. On the one hand, the privatization of the pipes had opened up a booming ISP market, serving the flood of people trying to get online: there were nearly 45 million users in 1995, up 76 percent from the year before. But getting people online was a small fraction of the system's total profit potential. What really got investors' blood and capital flowing was the possibility of making money from what people *did* online.

But how exactly? The internet may have been attracting millions of newcomers, but it still felt like a research network. The World Wide Web was its most accessible region—far friendlier than more technical and text-bound interfaces like Gopher and Usenet—but that wasn't saying much. The average site was hideous and barely usable. Finding content wasn't particularly easy: you could wander from one site to another by following the tissue of hyperlinks that connected them, or page through the handmade directory produced by Yahoo!, the preferred web portal before the rise of the modern search engine. And there wasn't much content to find: only 23,500 websites existed in 1995, compared to more than 17 million five years later.

But the smallness and slowness of the early web also lent it a certain charm. It remained a very personal place. People were excited to be there, despite there being relatively little for them to do. They made homepages simply to say hello, to post pictures of their pets, to share their enthusiasm for Star Trek. They wanted to connect.

Omidyar was fond of this form of online life. He had been a devoted user of the internet since his undergraduate days, and a participant in its various communities. He now observed the rising flood of dot-com money with some concern. The corporations clambering onto the internet saw people as nothing more than "wallets and eyeballs," he later told a journalist. Their efforts at commercialization weren't just crude and uncool; they also promoted a zombie-like passivity—look here, click here, enter your credit card number here—that threatened the participatory nature of the internet he knew.

"I wanted to do something different," Omidyar later recalled, "to give the individual the power to be a producer as well as a consumer." This was the motivation for the website he built during Labor Day weekend in 1995. He called it AuctionWeb. Anyone could put up something for sale, anyone could place a bid, and the item went to the highest bidder. It would be a perfect market in the sense that it would conform to the neoclassical ideal found in an economics textbook: through the miracle of competition, supply and demand would meet to discover the true price of a commodity. One precondition of perfect markets is that everyone has access to the same information, and this is exactly what AuctionWeb promised. Everything was there for all to see.

The site grew quickly. By its second week, the items listed for sale included a Yamaha motorcycle, a Superman lunchbox, and an autographed Michael Jackson poster. By February 1996, traffic had grown brisk enough that Omidyar's web hosting company increased his monthly fee, which led him to start taking a cut of the transactions to cover his expenses. Almost immediately, he was turning a profit. The side project had become a business.

But the perfect market turned out to be less than perfect. Disputes broke out between buyers and sellers, and Omidyar was frequently called upon to adjudicate. He didn't want to have to play referee, so he came up with a way to help users work it out themselves: a forum. People would leave feedback on one another, creating a kind of scoring system. "Give praise where it is due," he said in a letter posted to the site, "make complaints where appropriate." The dishonest would be driven out, and the honest would be rewarded—but only if users did their part. "This grand hope depends on your active participation," he wrote.

The value of AuctionWeb would rely on the contributions of its users. The more they contributed, the more useful the site would be. The market would be a community, a place made by its members. They would become both consumers and producers, as Omidyar hoped, and among the things they produced would be the content that filled the site.

By the summer of 1996, AuctionWeb was generating $10,000 a month. Omidyar decided to quit his day job and devote himself to it full-time. He had started out as a critic of the e-commerce craze and had ended up with a successful e-commerce company. In 1997, he renamed it eBay.

Platforms Don't Exist

eBay was one of the first big internet companies. It became profitable early, grew into an eminence of the dot-com era, survived the implosion of the dot-com bubble, and still ranks among the largest e-commerce firms in the world. But what makes eBay particularly interesting is how, in its earliest incarnation, it anticipated many of the key features that would later define the phenomenon commonly known as the "platform."

None of the metaphors we use to think about the internet are perfect, but "platform" is among the worst. The term originally had a specific technical meaning: it meant something that developers build applications on top of, such as an operating system or a set of application programming interfaces (APIs). But the word has since come to refer to various kinds of software that run online, particularly those deployed by the largest tech firms. As the scholar Tarleton Gillespie argues, this slippage is strategic. By calling their services "platforms," companies like Google can project an aura of openness and neutrality. They can present themselves as playing a supporting role, merely facilitating the interactions of others. Their sovereignty over the spaces of our digital life, and their active role in ordering such spaces, is obscured. It's no exaggeration to say, then, that platforms don't exist. The word isn't just imprecise; it's an illusion. It's designed to mystify rather than clarify.

As an alternative, consider the following starting point: our experience of the internet is organized by a set of complex systems that, despite considerable variation, share certain common characteristics. The best way to understand these systems is to historicize them—more specifically, to place them within the broader history of the internet's privatization.

The privatization of the internet began in the basement, with the pipes; by the mid-1990s, this phase was complete. The next step was figuring out how to maximize profit in the upper floors: the application layer, where users actually use the internet, which in the mid-1990s mostly meant the World Wide Web.

This was the central focus of the dot-com boom that began with Netscape's explosive IPO in August 1995. Over the following years, tens of thousands of startups were founded and hundreds of billions of dollars were invested in them. Venture capital entered a manic state: the total amount of investment increased more than 1,200 percent from 1995 to 2000. Hundreds of dot-com companies went public and promptly soared in value: at their peak, technology stocks were worth more than $5 trillion.

Yet profits mostly failed to materialize. This was partly intentional: the stated strategy of many dot-com companies was to grow fast and monetize later. But it also reflected a deeper difficulty. As Ed Horowitz, the CEO of Viacom, explained in 1996: "The Internet has yet to fulfill its promise of commercial success. Why? Because there is no business model." Horowitz was exaggerating slightly: eBay was profitable, for instance. But it was an exception to the general trend. Many of the dot-com companies that were driving the Nasdaq into a frenzy were nowhere close to being profitable. Even those that were had little chance of catching up to the stratospheric valuations the market had bestowed on them. The Nasdaq's average price-earnings ratio, which measures the relationship between a company's stock price and its earnings per share, had exceeded 200 by 1999. This meant investors were willing to pay $200 for every dollar of profit.

The next year, the bubble burst. From March to September 2000, the 280 stocks in the Bloomberg U.S. Internet Index lost almost $1.7 trillion. "It's rare to see an industry evaporate as quickly and completely," a CNN journalist remarked. And 2001 brought more bad news. The dot-com era was dead.

Today, the era is typically remembered as an episode of collective insanity—as an exercise in what Alan Greenspan, during his contemporaneous tenure as Fed chairman, famously called "irrational exuberance." Pets.com, a startup that sold pet supplies online, became the best-known symbol of the period's stupidity, and a touchstone for retrospectives ever since. Never profitable, the company spent heavily on advertising, including a Super Bowl spot; it raised $82.5 million in its IPO in February 2000 and imploded nine months later.

But it would be a mistake to see the failure of the dot-com experiment in purely personal terms. Arrogance, greed, magical thinking, and bad business decisions were all present in abundance. Yet none of these were decisive. The real problem was structural. While their investors and executives probably wouldn't have understood it in these terms, dot-com companies were trying to advance the next stage of the internet's privatization: namely, by pushing the privatization of the internet up the stack. But the elements that could make such a push feasible were not yet in place. With the pipes, the process had been relatively smooth: ISPs sold access. The dot-com entrepreneurs faced a larger challenge: they had to find a way to monetize *activity* rather than access. It's not that their ideas for doing so were all bad—in fact, many of the same ideas would resurface in later years to become the basis of highly valued businesses—but that the internet as it then existed couldn't accommodate them. A renovation was required.

In his analysis of capitalist development, Karl Marx drew a distinction between the "formal" and "real" subsumption of labor by capital. In formal subsumption, an existing labor process remains intact, but is now performed on a capitalist basis. For example, a peasant who used to grow his own food becomes a wage laborer on somebody else's farm. The way he works the land stays the same. In real subsumption, by contrast, the labor process is revolutionized to meet the requirements of capital. Formerly, capital inherited a process; now, it remakes the process. Our agricultural worker becomes integrated into the industrialized apparatus of the modern factory farm. The way he works completely changes: his daily rhythms bear little resemblance to those of his peasant predecessors. And the new arrangement is more profitable for the farm's owner, having been explicitly organized with that end in mind.

This is a useful lens for thinking about the evolution of the internet, and for understanding why the dot-coms didn't succeed. The internet of the mid-to-late 1990s was under private ownership, but it had not yet been optimized for profit. It retained too much of its old shape, and its old shape wasn't conducive to the new demands being placed on it. Formal subsumption had been achieved, in other words, but real subsumption remained elusive.

Accomplishing the latter would involve developments at a variety of levels—technical, social, economic—that made it possible to construct new kinds of systems. These systems are the digital equivalents of the modern factory farm. They represent the long-sought solution to the problem that consumed and ultimately defeated the dot-com entrepreneurs: how to push privatization up the stack. And eBay offered the first glimpse of what that solution looked like.

The Ultimate Market

eBay enlisted its users in its own creation. The site didn't just offer a space for their activities—it was constituted by them. They were the ones posting items for sale and placing bids and writing feedback on one another in the forum. Without their contributions, the site would cease to exist.

There was a tradition being tapped into here. The internet, when it was invented in the 1970s as a universal language that enabled different networks to interconnect, was originally designed to link stationary mainframes with mobile military forces. Yet what the internet became used for, as it evolved from an experiment into an institution, was something rather different. In the near term, it would not be used by mobile military forces; neither would it be primarily about sharing computing resources. Rather, its real value was social. The internet survived, and grew, because it gave people a way to communicate.

In this, the internet followed in the footsteps of its precursor, ARPANET. The pioneering computer network had also been created for the purpose of resource sharing. Then, in 1971, a programmer named Ray Tomlinson came up with email. Email became wildly popular: two years later, a study commissioned by DARPA's director found that it made up three-quarters of all network traffic. As the internet grew through the 1980s, email found an even wider reach. The ability to exchange messages instantaneously with someone far away was immensely appealing; it made new kinds of collaboration and conversation possible, particularly through the mailing lists that formed the first online communities.

Email was more than just a useful tool, though; it represented a kind of spiritual transformation. Email helped humanize the internet. It made a cold assemblage of cables and computers feel inhabited. The internet was somewhere you could catch up with friends and get into acrimonious arguments with strangers. It was somewhere to talk about politics or science fiction or the best way to implement a protocol. Other people were the main attraction, and this quality would endure, and inspire new applications, as the internet expanded. Even the World Wide Web was made with community in mind. "I designed it for a social effect—to help people work together," its creator, Tim Berners-Lee, would later write.

Community is what Omidyar liked best about the internet, and what he feared the dot-com gold rush would kill. He wasn't alone in this: one could find dissidents polemicizing against the forces of commercialization on radical mailing lists like Nettime. But Omidyar was no anti-capitalist. He was a libertarian: he believed in the liberating power of the market. He didn't oppose commercialization as such, just the particular form it was taking. The companies opening cheesy digital storefronts and plastering the web with banner ads were doing commercialization poorly because they didn't understand the internet. They didn't understand that it was a social medium.

eBay, by contrast, would be firmly rooted in this fact. From its first days as AuctionWeb, the site described itself as a community, and this self-definition became integral to its identity and to its operation. For Omidyar, the point wasn't to defend the community from the market but rather to recast the community *as a market*—to fuse the two.

This wasn't an entirely original idea. No less a figure than Bill Gates saw the future of the internet in precisely these terms. In 1995, the same year that Omidyar launched AuctionWeb, Gates co-authored a book called *The Road Ahead*. In it, the Microsoft CEO laid out his vision for the internet as "the ultimate market":

> It will be where we social animals will sell, trade, invest, haggle, pick stuff up, argue, meet new people, and hang out. Think of the hustle and bustle of the New York Stock Exchange or a farmers' market or of a bookstore full of people looking for fascinating stories and infor- mation. All manner of human activity takes place, from billion-dollar deals to flirtations.

Here, social relationships have merged so completely with market relationships as to become indistinguishable. The internet is the instrument of this union; it brings people together, but under the sign of capital. Gates didn't think this was imminent, however. On the contrary: he believed his dream was many years from being realized. Yet by the time his book came out, AuctionWeb was already making progress toward achieving it.

Community Standards

Combining the community with the market was a lucrative innovation. The interactions that occurred in the guise of the former greatly enhanced the value of the latter. Under the banner of community, AuctionWeb's buyers and sellers were encouraged to perform unpaid activities that made the site more useful, such as rating one another in the feedback forum or sharing advice on shipping. And the more people participated, the more attractive a destination it became. This was the first reason for the site's success: network effects.

Network effects occur when a good or service becomes more valuable the more people use it. More people using AuctionWeb meant more items listed for sale, more buyers bidding in auctions, more feedback posted to the forum—in short, a more valuable site. On the web, accommodating this growth was fairly easy: increasing one's hosting capacity was a simpler and cheaper proposition than the brick-and-mortar equivalent. And doing so was well worth it because, at a certain size, network effects locked in advantages that were hard for a competitor to overcome.

A second, related strength was the site's role as a middleman. In an era when many dot-coms were selling goods directly—Pets.com paid a fortune on postage to ship pet food to people's door—Omidyar's company connected buyers and sellers instead. This enabled it to profit from their transactions while remaining extremely lean. It had no inventory, no warehouses—just a website.

But both the benefits of being a middleman and those associated with network effects required a third factor as their enabling condition: a certain kind of sovereignty. The site didn't just facilitate interactions; it shaped them. It wrote the rules for how people could interact and designed the spaces where they did so. It was not only an intermediary but a legislator and an architect. This wasn't in Omidyar's initial plan. But it soon became a necessity, as the sociologist Keyvan

Kashkooli explores in his study of eBay's evolution. Omidyar's initial vision was of a market run by its members, an ideal informed by his libertarian beliefs. His decision to create the feedback forum likely reflected an ideological investment in the idea that markets were essentially self-organizing, as much as his personal interest in no longer having to mediate various disputes.

This laissez-faire approach broke down pretty quickly, however. Contrary to libertarian assumptions, the market couldn't function without something like a state. The feedback forum is a good example: users started manipulating it, leaving praise for their friends and sending mobs of malicious reviewers after their enemies. The company would be compelled to intervene again and again, not only to manage the market but also to expand it—an imperative that shareholders imposed after eBay went public in 1998. "Despite its initial reluctance, the company stepped increasingly into a governance role," writes Kashkooli. Preserving and increasing profitability required managing people's behavior, whether through the code that steered them through the site or the user agreements that governed their activities on it.

These three elements—sovereign, middleman, and maker of network effects—formed a powerful synthesis. Through them, the fusion of the market and the community would be achieved, and a surge of revenue unlocked. At a time when most dot-coms failed to turn a profit, eBay did so easily. When the crash of 2000–2001 hit, it survived with few bruises. And in the aftermath of the crash, as an embattled industry, under pressure from investors, tried to reinvent itself, the ideas that it came up with had much in common with those that had formed the basis for eBay's early success.

For the most part the influence was neither conscious nor direct. But the affinities were unmistakable. Omidyar's community market of the mid-1990s was an aperture into the future. By later standards it was fairly primitive, existing as it did within the confines of an internet not yet remodeled for the purpose of profit maximization. But the systems that would accomplish that remodeling, that qualitative leap from formal to real subsumption, that more total privatization of the internet, would do so by elaborating the basic patterns that Omidyar had applied. These systems would be called platforms, but what they resembled most were shopping malls.

6

Online Malls

Back in 1993, the activist Jeffrey Chester had warned that the information superhighway would become "a virtual electronic shopping mall" if corporate interests had their way. These were prescient words. He was right, and the metaphor he used was particularly fitting. If the firms that own the pipes of the internet are best understood as slumlords—gouging users while letting their infrastructure rot—then the systems that dominate life at the upper end of the stack are best understood, to borrow an insight from the scholar Jathan Sadowski, as shopping malls.

The first modern shopping mall was built in Edina, Minnesota, in 1956. Its architect, Victor Gruen, was a Jewish socialist from Vienna who had fled the Nazis and disliked American car culture. He wanted to lure midcentury suburbanites out of their Fords and into a place that recalled the "rich public social life" of a great European city. He hoped to offer them not only shops but libraries and theaters and community centers. Above all, his mall would be a space for interaction: an "outlet for that primary human instinct to mingle with other humans." Unlike in a city, however, this mingling would take place within a controlled setting. The chaos of urban life would be displaced by the discipline of rational design.

As Gruen's invention caught on, the grander parts of his vision would fall away. But the idea of an engineered environment that paired commerce with a public square remained. Gruen's legacy would be a kind of capitalist terrarium, nicely captured by the phrase "privately owned public space."

The shopping malls of the internet are nothing if not privately owned public spaces. They are corporate enclosures with a wide range of interactions transpiring inside of them. Just like in a real mall, some of these interactions are commercial, such as buying clothes from a merchant, while others are social, such as hanging out with friends. But what distinguishes the online mall from the real mall is that within the former, everything one does makes data. Every move, however small, leaves a digital trace. And these traces present an opportunity to create a completely new set of arrangements.

Real malls are in the rental business: the owner charges tenants rent, essentially taking a slice of their revenues. Online malls can make money more or less the same way, as eBay demonstrated early on, by taking a cut of the transactions they facilitate. But, as Sadowski points out, online malls are also able to capture another kind of rent: *data* rent. In other words, they can collect those digital traces generated by the activities that occur within them. And since they control every square inch of the enclosure, and because modifying the enclosure is simply a matter of deploying new code, they can introduce architectural changes as needed in order to cause those activities to generate more traces, or traces of different kinds.

These traces turn out to be quite valuable. So valuable, in fact, that amassing and analyzing them have become the primary functions of the online mall. Like Omidyar's community market, the online mall is a middleman, a sovereign, and a maker of network effects. It facilitates interactions, it writes the rules for those interactions, and it benefits from having more people interact. But in the online mall, these interactions are recorded and interpreted. This is what distinguishes online malls from their precursors. They are above all designed for making, and making use of, data. Data is their organizing principle and essential ingredient.

Data is sometimes compared to oil, but a better analogy might be coal. Coal was the fuel that powered the steam engine. It propelled the capitalist reorganization of manufacturing from an artisanal to an industrial basis, from the workshop to the factory, in the nineteenth century. Data has played a comparable role. It has propelled the capitalist reorganization of the internet, banishing the remnants of the research network and perfecting the profit engine. This process has been neither simple nor quick. It has taken time and it has taken different forms. Its origins are fairly easy to identify, however. It is closely linked to the rise of the company that, perhaps more than any other, is synonymous with the modern internet, and the only one whose name is used as a verb and is listed, lowercase, in the dictionary.

The Eyeball Business

In 1998, the same year that eBay burst onto the Nasdaq, a pair of graduate students presented a paper at an academic conference. The paper described a search engine they had built at Stanford. It was still a prototype—it ran on a set of scavenged and thrifted computers in a dorm room—but a prototype that had become so popular that, at peak times, it used half of the university's internet bandwidth. The students called it Google. That year, they founded a company of the same name.

The story of Google has been told many times before. It has been celebrated and emulated, critiqued and parodied. But what has receded in the telling and retelling of this story is the original problem that the young Larry Page and Sergey Brin were trying to solve. This is the problem of having too much data.

Having too much data was one of many scenarios unforeseen by the internet's architects. The idea that someday there would be billions of people and tens of billions of devices all bound together through the protocol they were creating was well beyond imagining. Their best guess at the outer bound of how many IP addresses they would ever need—the unique identifiers assigned to computers connected to the internet— was about 4.3 billion. Even that seemed excessive to some: the programmer Virginia Strazisar Travers, who played a central role in the internet's creation, later remembered thinking that 65,536 would be enough for her lifetime.

In the 1990s, the situation looked different. Tens of millions of people were joining the internet each year. Millions of miles of fiber-optic cable were being laid. And prodigious amounts of data were being manufactured, particularly on the World Wide Web, where newcomers congregated. The number of websites grew nearly 1,000 percent from 1995 to 1996.

In theory, more information should have made the web more useful. In practice, more information made the web more bewildering. The existing tools for making sense of it all simply weren't up to the job. Yahoo!'s reliance on humans—the fact that its listings were manually curated—meant that it struggled to keep pace with the growth of the web. Automated alternatives existed—"web crawlers" that indexed sites to make them searchable—but they weren't very good, often returning useless and spammy results.

This was the challenge that Page and Brin aimed to overcome, with funding from DARPA and the National Science Foundation—the agency that had created the internet and the agency that had run it until recently. "The number of documents in the [search engine] indices has been increasing by many orders of magnitude," they wrote in their 1998 paper, "but the user's ability to look at documents has not." Their solution was an algorithmic method for ranking the quality and relevance of a webpage that relied primarily on counting how many other sites linked to it. This tended to produce more pertinent results and, crucially, it scaled well. A vast and rapidly expanding patchwork would be made more intelligible through an automated analysis of how it was all sewn together.

But as Google moved off-campus and became a business and grew, something else happened. It began not only to organize the data of the web but to generate a fair bit of its own. Everything that users did left footprints in the servers' logs: what they searched for, when they searched for it, what results they clicked on, whether they stayed there or returned to start a new search. And the footprints added up: by November 1999, Google was processing more than 4 million searches a day.

The company began using this data to improve its search engine. By studying user behavior, engineers could identify gaps and glitches in the software, and remake the ranking algorithm to respond to a range of new signals. Then, in the early 2000s, the company started using the data for another purpose: to sell ads.

Google had been selling ads since 1999, though not very well. Sheryl Sandberg, a former Clinton administration staffer hired to lead the ads team, would later remember then-CEO Eric Schmidt walking by her desk multiple times a day to ask how many advertisers they had. Her answer was always the same: "Not many." The wounds were largely self-inflicted. Page and Brin hated online advertising, sharing Pierre Omidyar's distaste for the tacky commercialization of the dot-com era. Moreover, advertising wasn't central to the business model: revenue was mostly expected to come from licensing Google's search technology to other sites. But enough revenue didn't materialize, and the dot-com implosion of 2000–2001 meant that Google, like every other unprofitable internet company, was under pressure from investors. One of these investors, the venture capitalist Michael Moritz, would remember feeling quite pessimistic at the time. "We really couldn't figure out the business model," he later recalled.

This changed in 2002, the year that Google became profitable. The breakthrough involved AdWords, a system for selling and displaying ads. First, advertisers submitted bids on particular search terms, like "cars," "clothes," or something more specific. Then the system automatically selected the winner and placed its ad in the best spot on the search results page—the one the user was most likely to see—the ad of the runner-up in the second-best spot, and so on. But it wasn't just an auction: the bids weren't the only factor that determined ad placement. The other factor was a quality score computed for each ad, and this score was so important that it could catapult an advertiser into the top spot even if it didn't have the highest bid.

How was the quality score calculated? This was where those footprints in the servers' logs became useful. User data held lessons about the ad's relevance: the more users who clicked the ad, the more relevant the ad was assumed to be. The "click-through rate" thus became the initial measure of ad quality. Over time, ad quality would become a far more complex calculation, incorporating a number of different metrics and employing advanced statistical techniques known as "machine learning." Still, the basic idea remained the same. The company would observe user behavior in order to try to predict user behavior. If Google began as an attempt to interpret the abundant information of the web, its commercial viability would rest on interpreting the abundant information of its users.

The beauty of the arrangement is that it served both God and Mammon, which is to say, both Google's founders and investors. The quality score helped soften Page and Brin's antipathy to advertising, because it ensured that even a deep-pocketed advertiser couldn't flood the site with spam. There were guardrails. But these same guardrails also guided users to ads they were more likely to click on, which pleased advertisers. Money poured in and the investors were happy.

In *The Age of Surveillance Capitalism*, Shoshana Zuboff describes this moment as a turning point not only in the history of Google but in the history of capitalism. In her view, the discovery of "behavioral surplus"—a trove of user data so rich and plentiful that it could be put to work selling ads and not just improving search—gave birth to a new economic logic called "surveillance capitalism." "Google had discovered a way to translate its nonmarket interactions with users into surplus raw material for the fabrication of products aimed at genuine market transactions with its real customers: advertisers," she writes. "The corporation thus created out of thin air and at zero marginal cost an asset class of vital raw materials derived from users' nonmarket online behavior."

This wasn't the first time that companies had profited from personal data. Long before the internet became a mass medium, marketing firms, insurance companies, and others had been using computers to collect and analyze information about consumers, as the pioneering scholar of surveillance studies Oscar H. Gandy Jr. has documented. Still, the mainstreaming of the internet significantly enlarged the surface area for such surveillance, since everything that people did online made data. The successful monetization of this data at Google in the early 2000s may not have spawned a new form of capitalism—the pursuit of profit looked very much like the old capitalism—but it did mark a departure.

The nature of the novelty lay in Google's ability to derive value from data. Data was fabricated through Google's role as a middleman—connecting users to websites—and this data, when aggregated and analyzed, in turn made it possible for Google to play another middleman role—connecting advertisers to users. This latter activity benefited from network effects, because the more data users generated by using the site, the more could be learned about how best to serve them ads. And the company could use its power over the interactions occurring on the site—its sovereignty—to accelerate this learning process, and to induce users to make more of the data essential to it.

In short, in the early 2000s, Google became the first online mall. In the aftermath of the dot-com bust, it developed a digital enclosure of the kind that would, in the coming years, bring about the next phase in the privatization of the internet, the task that the dot-coms attempted but never achieved.

Making Friends

The innovations of 2002 were crude compared to what came later. Spying on people in order to sell ads would become a more sophisticated, and invasive, affair. It would feed on diverse data streams, from browsing history to credit card history to any number of subtler but often quite informative imprints that we scatter across the digital environments that envelop our lives. Such advertising would also spread throughout the web, and spawn a densely populated and extremely convoluted ecosystem—"black boxes inside of black boxes inside of black boxes" is how the journalist Shoshana Wodinsky describes it—of firms that facilitate the split-second auctions whereby advertisers compete to show an ad in a particular space on a particular site to a particular individual whose data trail suggests they might purchase a particular product.

Google remains the apex predator of this ecosystem, claiming 28.9 percent of the US digital ad market in 2020. The next-biggest player, which controls another 25.2 percent, is Facebook. Founded shortly after Google began its ad-fueled ascent, Facebook was part of a wave of startups that together came to define what we now know as "social media." The first iteration of Mark Zuckerberg's creation appeared in 2004, YouTube arrived in 2005 (and was purchased by Google the following year), and Twitter followed in 2006.

What characterized these sites was a reliance on user-generated content. At the time, tech guru Tim O'Reilly hailed this aspect as one of the pillars of what he called "Web 2.0": a new, more participatory web that emerged from the wreckage of the dot-com era. "The key to competitive advantage in internet applications is the extent to which users add their own data to that which you provide," he advised. "Involve your users both implicitly and explicitly in adding value to your application." This wasn't a new idea—as we've seen with eBay—but social media increased its significance, and made it the basis of new kinds of digital enclosures.

These enclosures would be particularly well suited to the business model popularized by Google, because their social nature encouraged users to offer up more data about themselves—data that could in turn be applied to the task of ad targeting. In the case of Facebook, the line of transmission was direct: in 2008, Zuckerberg hired Sheryl Sandberg, who had overseen Google's transformation into an advertising company, as his chief operating officer. Sandberg thus became, in Shoshana Zuboff's memorable phrase, "the 'Typhoid Mary' of surveillance capitalism."

The online mall of social media would look a bit different than the online mall of search. The goal would be to keep users locked inside of it as long as possible: to maximize "engagement," as executives would tell their engineers. Engagement might take many forms—a like, a retweet, a view, a share, a comment, a post—and these forms needed to be, on the one hand, flexible enough to accommodate a satisfying range of expression—for social media to work, it must feel genuinely social—but structured enough to be easily interpretable by software. As the theorist Philip E. Agre once observed, computers must impose a "grammar" on human activity to make it intelligible, just as the grammar of the English language makes it intelligible to its speakers.

A grammar is not a straitjacket, however; it is a remarkably supple thing. "Just as the speakers of English can produce a potentially infinite variety of grammatical sentences from the finite means of English vocabulary and grammar," Agre writes, "people engaged in captured activity can engage in an infinite variety of sequences of action, provided these sequences are composed of the unitary elements and means of combination prescribed by the grammar of action." In other words, one of the virtues of a grammar is the sense of freedom it allows. This sense of freedom helps explain why people find social media pleasurable. Even as their interactions are being subtly (or unsubtly) structured by the design of the user interface and the code underneath, they enjoy a feeling of autonomy, a feeling of being free to express themselves.

The power of the social media mall thus rests on a strange kind of sovereignty: the sort that pretends it doesn't exist. This disavowal has its legal basis in the famous Section 230, passed into law as part of the Communications Decency Act of 1996. Section 230 shields online services of all kinds, as well as ISPs, from legal liability for the speech they circulate. The protection it affords is especially vital for the owners of social media malls, who can disclaim responsibility for the activities of their users even as they are covertly involved in shaping those activities.

Only in exceptional circumstances—a high-profile user is banned, an obtrusive new feature is introduced—does the sovereign reveal himself. Most of the time, the "community" appears to organize itself. It is essential to the success of the social media mall that users behave as if their behavior is entirely their own, while being induced to behave in ways that are maximally legible to the automated systems that track and analyze them, ultimately for the purpose of selling ads.

Just because these ads are being displayed does not mean that people are paying attention to them, however. This is a crucial point. As the writer Tim Hwang explains, "advertising *packages* attention: it is not the attention itself." The attention itself is surprisingly hard to come by: a substantial body of research suggests that online advertising doesn't work particularly well. Widespread fraud, the rising popularity of ad blockers, a growing indifference to ads, and persistent problems with "ad viewability"—the fact that ads are not always loaded in places where someone will see them—all contribute to what Hwang calls a "subprime attention crisis": the overvaluing of advertising relative to its underlying asset, attention.

Immense amounts of data are being synthesized in the online malls built by Google and Facebook, and metabolized in various ways to help match ads to eyeballs. Yet the complexity of this operation does not mean that the individuals behind those eyeballs are necessarily clicking on the ads, much less buying anything. It would be a mistake to suggest, as Shoshana Zuboff often does, that Zuckerberg and his fellow surveillance capitalists have built a mind-control machine. Zuckerberg may want his customers—advertisers—to believe he has a mind-control machine, but beneath the marketing hype is a somewhat less impressive reality.

This is not to downplay the technical intricacy of these systems, or the unprecedented state of affairs they have brought about. "Attention is commodified to an extent that it has not been in the past," Hwang writes. The machinery of online advertising "has enabled the bundling of a multitude of tiny moments of attention into discrete, liquid assets that can then be bought and sold frictionlessly in a global marketplace." But the commodities that circulate in this marketplace may be far less valuable than tech firms lead advertisers to believe.

If online advertising doesn't work as well as promised, though, it works exceedingly well for the people making the promises. As I write, the combined market capitalization of Facebook and Google's parent company, Alphabet, is approaching $3 trillion, and rising fast.

7

Elastic Empires

Advertising occupies a central place in the story of privatization moving up the stack. But creating a marketplace for
attention is only one chapter in this story. Tech companies
also had to figure out how to create something more old-
fashioned: a marketplace for goods.

This wasn't as easy as it looked. E-commerce had been the
great hope of the dot-com boom, and it fell hard in the crash.
Selling coffee or groceries or dog food on the web led to some of
the era's most notorious flops. The problem was cost: it was easy
enough to put a product catalog online, but logistics turned out
to be a nightmare. Warehousing and delivery were complicated
and expensive. The company that ultimately cracked the code
was Amazon. In doing so, it displaced eBay, the darling of
the dot-coms, and joined Google and Facebook as one of the
leviathans of the modern internet. Its business model would
look different than that of the search and social media giants,
but it resembled them in one key respect: its triumph was largely
due to its evolution into a "platform"—that is, an online mall.

Amazon opened its online bookstore in July 1995, a couple months before the website that would become eBay appeared. The two founders struck a clear contrast. Pierre Omidyar was a programmer with a ponytail pursuing a side project. His initial motivation—creating the perfect market—was essentially utopian. Jeff Bezos was a Wall Street hedge fund manager without a utopian bone in his body. He was pure calculation, relentless and methodical, the logic of capital personified. He saw a business opportunity with the internet and didn't want to miss it.

Yet an early observer would probably consider Omidyar the better businessman. He had set out to create the perfect market and had ended up with the perfect business. eBay printed money. The formula was simple: it charged sellers a fee while staying far away from fulfillment. Amazon, by contrast, shipped goods to customers. This meant large fixed costs, and lots of energy devoted to making its sprawling distribution network more efficient. "This is horrible," Meg Whitman, eBay's CEO, told Omidyar after taking a tour of an Amazon facility in 1998. "The last thing we'd ever want to do is manage warehouses like this."

Amazon's margins were made even thinner by the fact that it undercut competitors to grab market share. Low prices helped the company grow fast but further deferred profitability. This didn't matter much during the delirious 1990s, but when the bubble burst in 2000 and 2001, Amazon started to look like just another dot-com with a cash flow crisis. The stock price dropped. Employees and even some executives became demoralized. In these years, writes the journalist Brad Stone, "most observers not only dismissed the company's prospects but also began to doubt its chances of survival."

Amazon crawled out of the crash by doing a number of things, perhaps the most important of which was become more of a middleman—that is, more like eBay. This was ironic, given the company's early history. In 1997, Barnes & Noble sued Amazon for false advertising, arguing that its claim to be "the world's largest bookstore" was a lie because it was actually "a book broker." The suit was settled later that year for an undisclosed sum. Yet the allegation, arguably true at the time, would only become truer.

The first step came in the fall of 2000, when the company unveiled a new feature called Marketplace. Third-party sellers would now be able to list their goods on Amazon's product pages and, most significantly, compete against Amazon on price. This was a controversial move that set off some grumbling within the company, but it paid off: in the first four months, monthly gross sales of third-party merchandise more than tripled. In January 2002, Amazon announced its first profitable quarter, with third-party sales already accounting for 15 percent of all orders.

In the coming years, as Marketplace grew, Amazon began aggressively poaching sellers from eBay. Disoriented by these attacks and undermined by a series of bad business decisions, eBay stumbled. By 2007, the war was over, and Amazon had won. That year, the company reported $14.8 billion in sales, more than eBay and Barnes & Noble combined. The 2000s was the decade when e-commerce went mainstream: the percentage of American adults who had purchased something online more than doubled between 2000 and 2009. Amazon's streamlined storefront and obsessively optimized logistics network made it well positioned to harvest a large share of this spending, as internet shopping became less about late-night bidding wars over rare Beanie Babies and more about satisfying ordinary needs.

Building a third-party marketplace enabled Amazon to meet more of those needs by opening its site to millions of small and mid-sized businesses. By 2017, third-party sellers were responsible for most of the sales on the site. The revenue they represented for Amazon was substantial. They paid the company fees and, if they chose to have their orders fulfilled by Amazon, purchased warehousing and delivery services. They could also obtain financing, as Amazon began giving out business loans. Finally, they could be induced to buy ads that made their products more visible to customers, whether in searches or elsewhere on the site—a miniature marketplace for attention embedded within the marketplace for goods.

But third-party sellers didn't just pay in money. They also paid in data. Their activities were surveilled no less comprehensively than those of Amazon's customers. And this is where Amazon converged with Google and Facebook: its rise, like theirs, rested on the manufacture and processing of large quantities of information. "They happen to sell products," former executive James Thomson later told the BBC, "but they are a data company."

This identity had started to take shape in the late 1990s, as Jeff Bezos began placing greater emphasis on technology and hiring more technical people. Personalization became a priority. Software engineers created a system that used data about customers—what they bought, what they looked at—to generate automated product recommendations. Just like at Google around the same time, user behavior would be monitored in order to make automated predictions about what someone might buy. These predictions also informed how much of this or that item the company should stock in its warehouses and determined the optimal prices to set for those items. Data helped Amazon solve the logistics challenges that had been fatal for a number of dot-coms.

Adding the third-party marketplace greatly expanded the scope of these operations. The company could now observe not only buyers, but sellers as well. In fact, it could observe entire markets. It would become a proper online mall, facilitating interactions in order to create data about them. And this data would prove valuable in a variety of ways, not least as a market research tool for Amazon's own product lines.

When businesses sell through Marketplace, Amazon watches them closely. It records detailed information about sales, shipping, and marketing. Then it uses this information to launch its own copycat products. The third-party marketplace thus "functions as a petri dish" for Amazon, argues the legal scholar and current Federal Trade Commission chair Lina Khan, where "independent firms undertake the initial risks of bringing products to market and Amazon gets to reap from their insights, often at their expense." Amazon not only competes with sellers, in other words, it also uses their data against them. And since it controls the online mall, it can promote its own merchandise over those of its rivals. "That was something we did quite well," Randy Miller, former director of merchandise pricing and product management at Amazon, told the journalist Brad Stone. "If you don't know anything about the business, launch it through the Marketplace, bring retailers in, watch what they do and what they sell, understand it, and then get into it."

In the 1990s, Amazon was a promising if unprofitable dot-com. In the 2000s and 2010s, it became an empire of the modern internet, in large part by imitating its main competitor, and with a rigor and a ruthlessness that eBay never quite achieved. In doing so, Amazon not only created a marketplace for consumer goods in these years, it also created a marketplace for capital goods. Capital goods are the means of production. The means of production that Amazon sold would be the machinery needed to make software for a commercializing internet.

The Internet's Factories

When capitalism transforms something, it tends to add more machinery. The internet was no different. In the post-dot-com period, as firms began to find more promising paths to profitability, they also made the internet more complex. The simple static web page faded from view. In its place came the dynamic and interactive web *application*, designed to seize a user's attention and stimulate their engagement, linked to elaborate subterranean systems of data collection and analysis.

The online mall would be a computationally intensive affair. Just as the capitalist transformation of manufacturing meant replacing the workshop with the factory, the capitalist transformation of the internet would hatch factories of its own. These factories weren't generally considered factories, though. That's because they came to be known by a name that obscured their fundamentally industrial character: the cloud.

If the internet is a collection of machines that talk to one another, the cloud is the subset of machines that do most of the talking. More concretely, the cloud is a globally distributed set of climate-controlled buildings—"data centers"—filled with servers. These servers supply the storage and perform the computation for the software running on the internet. When you do something online, your computer—the one on your desk or the one in your pocket—is probably talking to the cloud. At its most basic level, the cloud is a computer being used by another computer through a network.

This is a surprisingly old idea. In the 1960s, the advent of "time-sharing" systems offered an early way to stretch computation over a network. Such systems enabled multiple users to run programs on a single mainframe simultaneously from individual terminals. This made computing more accessible at a time when computers were large and expensive. An entire industry sprung up around the concept, selling computer time by the hour to companies that couldn't afford to buy mainframes.

The on-demand model was so successful that experts predicted it would come to dominate the digital world. "Computing may someday be organized as a public utility," declared MIT computer scientist John McCarthy in 1961. A few years later, his business school colleague Martin Greenberger imagined an "information utility" that supplied computing on tap in much the same way as the power utility supplied electricity. In a slightly different mode, the desire to share computing resources through a network inspired both the making of ARPANET in the 1960s and the making of the internet in the 1970s. The goal of the internet, after all, was to stretch computation over not just one network but several: to make a global network of networks that let the soldier in the field run a program on a mainframe on the other side of the planet. This is the aspiration that, decades later, found its fulfillment in the creation of the modern cloud.

While the modern cloud has several points of origin, the company most closely associated with its creation is Amazon. It was within Amazon that the idea of constructing an on-demand computing service took root, yielding a very profitable line of business. Its cornerstone would be laid some ten thousand miles from Seattle, by a small team in a South African suburb.

Far from the Mothership

In 2004, an Amazon employee named Chris Pinkham took a flight to Cape Town. He had spent the past few years running the company's network infrastructure in Seattle. Now he was returning to South Africa, the country where he grew up, to open an office there with his colleague Christopher Brown. There was no real reason for Amazon to have an office in Cape Town. But Pinkham wanted to come home, and Bezos didn't want to lose him.

Pinkham and Brown set up shop in an office park that bordered Constantia, South Africa's oldest wine region. Back in the seventeenth century, the Dutch colonial governor had put his many slaves to work planting row after row of grape vines in the area. The wine made from them became famous in Europe; Napoleon ordered bottles of it from his exile on Saint Helena. Centuries later, the vineyards were still there, now lined with fancy restaurants that served dishes like quail confit. Inside the Amazon office the scene was somewhat less fancy. The furnishings were spare: an early hire remembers sitting on cardboard boxes instead of chairs. In this spartan setting, Pinkham and Brown hired a handful of engineers. Then they began building what would come to be known as Elastic Compute Cloud, or EC2.

Pinkham had joined the company in 2000, right in the middle of the dot-com meltdown. "Amazon had reached enormous scale but it suffered a lot of growing pains," he later recalled. Among the most painful was its internal infrastructure: the collection of servers its engineers used to run their software. That software had grown increasingly sophisticated over the years. By the early 2000s, Amazon was already deep in the data business, and was busy expanding its online mall of third-party sellers. But the practices that had grown up around these pursuits were chaotic. Developers in different corners of the company were constantly reinventing the wheel. "Jill on the third floor is doing the same thing, and Rick on the fifth floor is doing the same thing," is how current Amazon CEO Andy Jassy would later describe this period. "There was this real angst and frustration internally, and yearning for reliable, scalable, cost-effective infrastructure services."

So Amazon began to rationalize its digital innards. Various initiatives emerged to push this process forward. By the time Pinkham landed in Cape Town in late 2004, the company had coalesced around a plan. It would build an on-demand computing service—a cloud—not just for itself, but for the world. "Let's make it a new business," Bezos would later remember thinking. "We need to do it for ourselves anyway." They weren't the only ones feeling the pain. Plenty of other companies were also struggling with the core challenge of life after the dot-com crash: how to manage greater technical complexity while boosting revenue and lowering costs.

The team in Cape Town worked on EC2 through 2005 and much of 2006. The office grew a bit more respectable—they got desks—but the atmosphere remained pretty loose.

An early hire remembered seeing a developer walking around barefoot juggling when he first came in for an interview. There were advantages to being far from Seattle. Pinkham and the others could work in peace, untroubled by Bezos's notorious micromanaging. "I spent most of my time trying to hide from Bezos," Pinkham later recalled. "He was a fun guy to talk to but you did not want to be his pet project." Jesse Robbins, the engineer responsible for keeping Amazon's websites running smoothly from Seattle, would put it more starkly. "It might never have happened if they weren't so far away from the mothership," he said.

Far from the mothership, the developers assembled something that looked a lot like the information utility prophesied by the experts of the 1960s. They did so by drawing on a technique dating from the same period: virtualization. Virtualization is the art of tricking a computer into believing a simulated resource is real. This resource might be a hard drive or a whole computer. Either way, it is treated as if it were the genuine article—you might not be able to touch a virtual hard drive, but your computer can't tell the difference.

The developers in Cape Town used virtualization to pack physical servers full of virtual ones. The latter became the basic unit of EC2, which would enable customers to rent virtual servers. Virtualization had two big advantages. One was efficiency: when you stuffed a single physical computer with many virtual ones, you made better use of the underlying resources. This was why, by the mid-2000s, some companies had already begun using virtualization in their servers. But the other benefit, and the one that the Amazon developers put at the center of their offering, was scalability.

Spinning up a new virtual server was much easier than installing a new physical server. If your website suddenly experienced a surge of traffic, you could add more virtual machines with a few keystrokes. This was the reason they called it *Elastic* Compute Cloud: the infrastructure could quickly stretch to meet demand. Moreover, this elasticity made it easier to sell computing on a metered basis, like electricity or water or gas.

After a year and a half of development in Cape Town, EC2 launched in 2006. Following the same playbook as the e-commerce division, prices were kept low to drive growth: renting a fairly robust virtual server for an hour cost ten cents. Along with Simple Storage Service (S3), an online storage system released that same year, EC2 would be the flagship offering of Amazon Web Services (AWS). AWS created, and still dominates, the market for cloud infrastructure services.

Its arrival was well timed. The post-dot-com period, as Google demonstrated, would be about amassing data and finding a way to monetize it. AWS offered a relatively affordable set of tools for manufacturing, storing, organizing, and processing this precious resource. If pushing privatization up the stack meant, above all, remaking the internet into a field for data production, then AWS would furnish the machinery for such an endeavor. Its portfolio, which soon expanded beyond EC2 and S3 to include dozens of different services, would enable smaller, newer, or less technical companies to create online malls, and to develop some of the same capacities of a firm like Google without having to build their own infrastructure or acquire top engineering talent.

These dynamics accelerated with the onset of the "big data" era in the 2010s. This period saw rapid advances in machine learning, a set of techniques for pattern recognition that could be applied to a number of tasks with increasing precision, from predicting consumer preferences to understanding human speech to recognizing human faces. Because machine learning "learns" by training on data, the abundant amount of data being generated through the internet greatly sped the development of the technology. Online data-making became the indispensable precondition for the growth of automated systems that came to be associated with "artificial intelligence."

The sophistication of these systems, and the wealth and power they appeared to bestow on major tech firms, stimulated an even stronger and more generalized hunger for data. What the sociologists Marion Fourcade and Kieran Healy call the "data imperative" implanted itself throughout the corporate world and in many government agencies. Organizations began to stockpile as much data as possible in the hopes of securing a little artificial intelligence of their own. Here too AWS could help, selling machine learning services in the cloud.

The Everywhere Machine

The birth of the online mall, the rise of the cloud, the spread of the data imperative—these were the principal vectors for the deeper privatization of the internet in the decade or two after the dot-com crash. But there was another change that profoundly altered the shape of the network: its diffusion.

The internet that knitted itself together over the course of the 1980s was stationary. People logged on from computer labs, typically at universities. In the 1990s, as the internet began to move into people's homes, it remained fixed in place, now tethered to the personal computer. A user from 1990 transported to 2005 would encounter a very different online world, but the interfaces through which they encountered that world would look much the same: a keyboard, mouse, and monitor.

The same individual transported to 2020 would find something less familiar. Over the course of the 2010s, the internet went mobile. In 2011, only 35 percent of Americans had a smartphone; by 2019, that number was 81 percent. At the same time, more objects acquired a network connection, from cars to thermostats to security cameras to industrial equipment. According to Cisco, this "Internet of Things" will account for fully half of all networked devices globally by 2023.

In the 1980s, the internet went from being a protocol to a place. In the 1990s and 2000s, that place grew massively. In the 2010s, it became a different kind of place altogether. It cut its tether, losing its anchorage in a fixed point. It became fluid, ubiquitous, diffuse. The internet was no longer something people logged onto but something that was always on: fastened to your hand or wrist or pocket, woven through homes and workplaces and cities. "Smartness" came to saturate the spaces of everyday life.

"Smartness" is best understood as an object's membership in an entire layer of computation that is bound together by the universal language of the internet. The "smartness" of an object is a function of the fact that it can talk to other computers, primarily those in the cloud. The cloud serves the applications and the data that make objects "smart," and soaks up the data that such objects continuously emit, which in turn feeds the machine learning systems that make the objects "smart" in the first place.

As a kind of networked intelligence, "smartness" belongs to a broader history of humans trying to make intelligent machines. An important figure in this history is the mathematician Alan Turing, who, in the 1930s, came up with the idea for a "universal machine." Using a limited set of logical operations, this hypothetical device could "be used to compute any computable sequence," Turing wrote. It could be programmed, in other words. Turing's concept became the basis for the modern computer. A machine is typically made for a particular task. By contrast, the computer is a universal machine because it is infinitely programmable. It can give us directions, prepare our tax returns, or simulate the collision of subatomic particles.

What if this universality became ubiquitous? What if machines that could do everything—or at least any computable task—were everywhere? If the computer is an everything machine, what happens when it becomes an everywhere machine? Sun Microsystems once had a slogan, credited to chief scientist John Gage: The network is the computer. The phrase has become infinitely truer than it was when it was first coined in the 1980s. The network is the computer, and the computer is everywhere.

Consider the "smart cooler" that Walgreens began using in its stores in 2019. The cooler is covered with bright digital screens. While a customer stands there trying to decide what to buy, a suite of sensors and cameras watches her. They track her irises to learn which products she's looking at. They take pictures of her face and send them to the cloud, where machine learning services try to determine her age and gender. All of this information goes into a database somewhere, to be analyzed by the retailer and the beverage companies. But it also has a more immediate effect. Maybe Diet Coke is running a promotion that targets young women, and the cloud has told the cooler that it thinks the person is a young woman. As a result, the digital screens that cover the cooler display an ad for Diet Coke. If she ends up buying one, the data point is duly recorded, another morsel to be stowed away for further analysis.

At least, this was the initial plan. In response to public outcry, the coolers never implemented the facial-recording or iris-tracking features. Rather, the ads would be keyed to variables like the weather or the time of day. Still, the story exemplifies a wider trend. The proliferation of "smartness" is aimed at making digital surveillance as deeply integrated into our physical world as it is in our virtual one. By putting internet-connected devices in more places, companies can put more of our lives online, which means more data about our lives can be manufactured. The CEO of the company behind the smart cooler cites Google as an inspiration: the goal is to bring the same advertising model to brick-and-mortar settings.

But, as with Google, it's debatable how effective such advertising is. "Smartness" always belongs in quotes because it rarely works exactly as promised; for one, it's impossible to determine someone's gender by scanning their face. Still, technologies don't have to work exactly as promised for the companies producing them to profit. And there is no doubt that the smartphone and the Internet of Things have opened new frontiers for profit-making. The major online malls have been central participants in, and beneficiaries of, the diffusion of the internet. Smartphones' geolocation data lets Google and Facebook promise more precise forms of targeting to advertisers. The Echo "smart speaker" lets Amazon learn more about its customers by placing listening devices in their living rooms. If the fiber-optic cables that traverse oceans and continents are the internet's arteries, these are its capillaries. They convey data through passages narrow and numerous enough to permeate nearly everything.

The irony of this phenomenon is that, while it represents a new stage in the evolution of the internet, it also represents something of a return. The DARPA researchers who created the protocol in the 1970s envisioned a network with mobile nodes. For the Pentagon to get the most out of its computers, Vint Cerf later said, "the computers have to be where the people are." The universal language of the internet would put the computers where the people were by making the mainframe accessible from the battlefield. And because the forces in the battlefield weren't fixed in place, the internet couldn't be either. This is why the experiments of the 1970s to prove the protocol's viability involved a van driving down the freeway, sending and receiving packets through the air.

Decades later, the internet is circling back to its founding idea. After an interlude as a network of fixed nodes, it is acquiring the flexibility, and ubiquity, originally imagined by its creators in the 1970s. As Cerf had hoped, the internet is putting the computers where the people are. Billions of connected objects are engaged in a perpetual conversation conducted in the lingua franca of the internet.

Command and Control

The XVIII Airborne Corps is a unit of the US Army designed to deploy anywhere in the world on short notice. This involves loading large airplanes with tanks, troops, and the other heavy things one needs to fight wars. Figuring out exactly how to load these planes is no small task. Making efficient use of the cargo bay is one consideration, but there are a number of others, such as whether the plane might land while taking enemy fire. Generating the optimal "load plan" is a complicated calculation.

In the late 1970s, DARPA thought the internet could help. At the time, making the load plan was a manual job. "Guys would run around with little stubby pencils and paper trying to figure it out," Vint Cerf later recalled. A group of DARPA contractors came up with an alternative. They put together a demonstration at Fort Bragg, North Carolina, home to the XVIII Airborne, that used the internet to automate the process. A computer sat on the tarmac, plugged into a packet radio. An operator sat at the computer and, through the new internet protocol, accessed a program running on another, larger computer connected to ARPANET. The operator entered the relevant data and the program returned the load plan. It took thirty seconds. Doing everything on paper took days.

This may have been the first time in history that a computer, speaking to another computer through the internet, told somebody what to do. It was an example of what we would now call "algorithmic management," and it shows that the purpose of linking the mainframe with the battlefield was that the mainframe could help *manage* the battlefield: DARPA's pitch to the Pentagon centered on the internet's usefulness for command and control in mobile environments. It would be many years before a truly mobile internet appeared, however. When it did, the possible future that briefly flickered into view on that day at Fort Bragg returned with it. As DARPA had predicted, the elasticity of the internet, its skill in conducting data across heterogeneous networks over large distances, made it a powerful tool for algorithmic management.

No company has fulfilled this prediction more energetically than Uber. Founded in 2009, it would be an online mall in the mold of Google, Facebook, and Amazon—though it didn't make a market in attention or in goods but rather in labor, matching customers who wanted a service performed with the workers who could perform it, on demand. Like any online mall, however, Uber isn't only or even primarily a middleman; it is also a sovereign. It facilitates interactions while exercising fine-grained control over the terms of those interactions, and this control goes far beyond that of a market-maker. In addition to setting rates for services—how much a ride costs in each city—it plays an intimate role in determining *how* services are performed. Software running in Uber's cloud directs the driver through a smartphone app. Just like at Fort Bragg, a computer, speaking to another computer through the internet, tells somebody what to do.

Sometimes this direction is quite direct. The app guides the driver along the optimal route for picking up and dropping off a passenger or a delivery, computed from factors like current and historical traffic patterns. Sometimes the direction is less direct: the app uses "surge pricing" to lure drivers into specific zones with the promise of higher rates, or displays messages that encourage drivers to keep driving when they're about to log off, or implements "gamified" design features that borrow behavioral insights from the psychology of slot machines to induce drivers to work longer hours. These are examples of what scholars Alex Rosenblat and Luke Stark call "soft control"—veiled but effective expressions of managerial authority.

Such techniques would be impossible without the copious quantities of data that Uber manufactures about its drivers. Drivers are observed just as closely as users within the digital enclosures of Google, Facebook, and Amazon. When they drive, how often their rides last, how fast they're going, how hard they hit the brakes—the app records all these data points, among many others, and transmits them to the cloud for analysis, which improves the algorithms further. The routes become more efficient. The nudges to persuade drivers to keep driving become more personalized.

Algorithmic management thus enables Uber and its many "gig economy" imitators to coordinate the labor of millions of workers without the need for middle managers, and with more technical sophistication than middle managers could ever achieve. Yet this is only one advantage. The other is that, by having software rather than humans telling workers what to do, and having the software use techniques like nudges and gamification, gig companies can pretend that nobody is telling the workers what to do, and therefore that they are not really workers at all. Uber refers to its drivers as "partners" or "entrepreneurs"; legally speaking, they are "independent contractors," at least in the United States. This classification is a pillar of the gig-work business model, since it holds down labor costs by preventing firms from having to pay a minimum wage or comply with the other legal protections afforded to direct employees. "In the US, direct employment increases corporate costs by roughly one-third, so classifying workers as independent contractors significantly increases profitability," notes Veena Dubal, a legal scholar who studies the gig economy.

Precisely for this reason, companies of all different kinds have spent the past several decades outsourcing wherever possible. This has created what labor market expert David Weil calls the "fissured workplace": rather than hiring workers directly, firms increasingly parcel out work to contractors. Uber is far from the first to embrace this model, and far from the first to combine this model with the internet. In fact, the internet is closely associated with the rise of contracting. The technology turned out to be an indispensable instrument for the fissuring of the workplace.

Discipline at a Distance

Networks are good at moving work around. As soon as corporate offices became networked in the early 1990s, executives began using them to reorganize their workforce. Wide area networks (WANs) spanning multiple sites let firms relocate "back-office" functions like data processing to places with lower labor and real estate costs. Then, as these networks became connected to the wider internet, such functions could be pushed even farther out and, increasingly, overseas.

Networking "supported organizations that wanted to divide their labor force geographically," writes the political economist Joan Greenbaum. And not only geographically: as certain kinds of work were displaced from the corporate core, they were also outsourced. The directly employed customer service representative became a subcontracted call-center operator in another country.

In this respect, the internet resembles the shipping container, the simple metal box that revolutionized global logistics in the 1960s and 1970s. The shipping container made it cheaper to transport goods by streamlining and mechanizing what had formerly been a time-consuming and labor-intensive process, and this in turn enabled companies to farm out their manufacturing operations to subcontractors in whatever parts of the world goods could be most cheaply produced. And what the shipping container has done to much blue-collar work, the internet has done to much white-collar work.

It "has created a massive globalized reservoir of human labor power for companies to tap into, as much or as little as needed: the 'human cloud,'" writes scholar Gavin Mueller. This human cloud includes the immense "back office" maintained by large tech companies, which use freelance and subcontracted workers in low-wage countries to categorize data sets so that machine learning algorithms can learn to detect patterns from them. A "smart" system is able to know what a horse looks like, for example, because it has trained on millions of photographs that have been labeled, by a human, as having horses in them.

If all the internet did was move work around, however, it wouldn't be nearly as useful. The trick with fissuring the workplace is that you have to find a way to retain a degree of control over the various fragments after you're finished fissuring. Exercising authority as an employer is relatively straightforward when your workforce is under your roof. But what happens when the office is decomposed into a global archipelago of contractors bound together by fiber-optic cable?

The internet makes it possible to manage this archipelago by enacting labor discipline at a distance: not only across physical distances, but also across the figurative distances of the fissured workplace. The same networks used to distribute work can also be used to surveil and supervise the workers doing it. In this respect, Uber is both representative of a broader trend and operating at its bleeding edge. The untethering of the internet has made it possible to put the human cloud everywhere. The humans can be provisioned wherever there is a smartphone signal and managed algorithmically through an app. The goal is a world where labor power can be conjured as painlessly as computing power, scaled to meet demand, and then discarded—a human cloud of virtual machines in which the virtual machines are people.

Real Abstractions

Uber is one of the main characters in the story of how privatization moved up the stack. The human cloud it created, and those it inspired, have helped remodel the internet for the market—putting Uber in the same category as Google, Facebook, Amazon, and the other major online malls. Unlike those firms, however, Uber doesn't turn a profit. Instead, it loses billions of dollars each year. No tech company, in fact, has ever lost quite so much. The whole point of privatizing the internet is to profit from it. Yet Uber and its gig economy peers are singularly unprofitable.

At one level, this bizarre state of affairs reflects the influence of venture capital, a popular form of financing that gives money to startups in exchange for equity. While venture is only one source of financing for tech companies—a larger share is made up from hedge funds, mutual funds, investment banks, and the bond and equity markets—it exerts special influence because of its close historical ties with the industry, and its influence can be seen in the way that many tech companies operate. As venture funds are designed to demand large returns, this hunger for hyperscale is passed on to start-ups in the form of an imperative to grow at any cost. Then, once the company has acquired enough market share, it can use its dominant position to achieve the profits that its investors require.

This was a popular strategy in the 1990s boom and one successfully pursued by Amazon, though it never burned through as much cash as Uber. But macroeconomic conditions in recent decades have made it even easier to source capital for such ventures. As the scholar Nick Srnicek points out, permanently low interest rates, the legacy of the Federal Reserve's response to the financial crisis of 2007–2008 and its very long aftermath, have reduced the returns on various financial assets. "The result is that investors seeking higher yields have had to turn to increasingly risky assets—by investing in unprofitable and unproven tech companies, for instance," he writes. Uber is a prime beneficiary, but it is far from the only one. A mere 18 percent of publicly traded startups valued at more than $1 billion were profitable in 2019. By comparison, about 80 percent of the firms that went public in the 1980s were profitable at the time of their IPO.

With so much money sloshing around, investors can afford to be patient. But what makes them believe their patience will be rewarded? In the case of Uber, this faith can be measured precisely: the company, despite losing billions, is worth tens of billions of dollars. Understanding how such a paradox is possible clarifies the nature of Uber's role in the privatization of the internet, and the further frontier of networked money-making it represents.

As an online mall, Uber collects both monetary rents and data rents. The monetary rents are the commissions that the company charges on each ride. These don't come close to covering its costs, which is why it loses money. The data rents are the manifold streams of information that Uber draws from its drivers, which are used to develop and refine the algorithms that manage their labor. But that's not all this data does. It also serves a psychological purpose: it helps persuade investors that Uber is worth a lot of money, despite being so unprofitable.

The data has both an operational value and a speculative financial value, in other words. And the two are connected. The reason that data "attracts venture capital and grows financial valuations" is because "investors expect data-rich platform companies to achieve competitive advantages by creating data-driven cost efficiencies, cross-industry synergies, and new markets," according to Niels van Doorn and Adam Badger, two academics who research the gig economy. The hope is that manufacturing large quantities of data through the internet will, through the magic of machine learning and other modes of analysis, lead to optimizations that boost revenue. For Van Doorn and Badger, data manufacturing is the heart of Uber's business model. Its human cloud is a factory for the production of financial value. The labor of drivers is directed at creating "data assets" that help secure the capital that allows the company to keep growing.

Whether this growth will ever result in profits is an open question. But even if it doesn't, plenty of individuals and institutions will have profited along the way. Uber's seed round, which refers to the first stage of fundraising, is "one of the greatest venture-capital investments of all-time," reports the *Wall Street Journal.* In 2010, the venture fund First Round Capital invested $510,000; at the time of Uber's IPO in 2019, its stake was worth $2.5 billion, a return of nearly 5,000 times. More than a few major shareholders have cashed out, locking in substantial gains. Goldman Sachs, an early investor, did so in late 2019, likely making hundreds of millions of dollars in profit. Around the same time, Uber co-founder Travis Kalanick did the same, liquidating more than $2.5 billion of stock.

Just because Uber is unprofitable doesn't mean that certain well-placed people can't profit from it. These are profits derived from speculation, not production. But in contemporary capitalism, profits from speculation are a primary means by which capital accumulation occurs. Since the 1970s, the US economy has become increasingly financialized. The financial sector has grown in size and significance while the productive sector has shrunk. Money made from moving other money around has become as important—perhaps even more important—as money made from making things. What Uber and other comparable companies offer, particularly in their early stages, are exceptionally lucrative linkages between financialization and the internet. Investors can ride a rising wave of paper wealth as the valuation of a firm grows, and then convert that paper wealth into real wealth during a "liquidity event" such as an IPO or an acquisition, regardless of whether the firm ever turns a profit. Data is an essential lubricant in this cycle, as it helps uphold investor confidence in the possibility of profitability.

SEN. Z

0359

September 19, 2022

33281930104754   Internet for the people

Saturation Point

Unprofitable tech companies acting as vehicles for speculation is a familiar theme—it was a major feature of the 1990s. But no dot-com was ever as unprofitable as Uber. Uber thus represents something new, a twist in the story of the internet's privatization.

We might sort that story into three phases: the ascendant, the triumphant, and the baroque. In the ascendant phase, the telecoms took control of the pipes and defeated any attempt to impose a degree of popular control, such as the proposal for a "public lane on the information superhighway." This victory laid the basis for the dot-com boom. The premise of the boom was that, with the pipes now safely in the hands of industry, privatization could be pushed up the stack.

It took longer than expected but, in the years after the dot-com bust, this objective was largely achieved. Online malls emerged to mediate a range of digital interactions while making data about them, and this data was monetized in a variety of ways. The rise of the cloud and the evolution of "big data" techniques like machine learning contributed valuable tools for organizing and analyzing data, while the diffusion of the internet through the smartphone and the Internet of Things opened new sites for manufacturing it. This was the triumphant phase, in which the internet was remade for the purpose of profit maximization and became the basis for some extraordinarily successful companies.

These companies were so successful, in fact, that investors became willing to plow unprecedented sums of money into startups in the hopes of finding the next one. Such startups could delay profitability while their valuation rose, enabling their shareholders to turn a profit when these companies went public or were acquired by a larger company. Acquisitions in particular increased as large tech firms began going on shopping sprees, using the ample cash holdings they had accrued through growing monopoly power and elaborate tax avoidance schemes. Startups were purchased for their technology or their personnel—or simply out of the concern that they might become competitors. Facebook has bought almost a hundred companies; Google, more than two hundred.

All of this adds a new dimension to the dynamics of data monetization. Data helps Google and Facebook sell ads and Amazon sell goods (and ads). But data helps Uber sell itself— which is to say, its equity. Data is converted into money through its interaction with the psychology of financial markets. This is the baroque phase of the internet's privatization, in which capital is so abundant and the potential returns so immoderate that investors can live on hope alone.

It would be easy to dismiss this behavior as irrational, comparable to the collective hallucinations that characterized the dot-com era. In some cases, there is no doubt that a similar level of self-delusion is at work. But as a whole, the internet is quite different than it was in the 1990s; for one, real business models have been built. In this sense, the achievements of the triumphant phase are the enabling condition for the excesses of the baroque phase. In 2020, the combined profits of Facebook, Amazon, and Google's parent company, Alphabet, hit $90 billion. Investors throwing money at startups may or may not succeed, but the sector now has a track record of real, and impressive, returns.

Moreover, there aren't a lot of other obvious places for capital to go. Tech is one of the few profit centers left in an economy that has been decelerating for decades. In the 1970s, GDP and labor productivity growth rates began falling, and it's been downhill ever since. This loss of dynamism wasn't limited to the US; the story in Western Europe and Japan was much the same. Each subsequent decade has marked further decline: these economies performed more poorly in the 1980s than in the 1970s, and more poorly in the 1990s than in the 1980s. The opening decades of the twenty-first century, with the Great Recession and the economic fallout of the COVID-19 pandemic, have been especially dismal. But stagnation, as the economist Thomas Piketty has shown, isn't bad for everyone. As the US economy has slowed down, it has also become more unequal: since the 1970s, the richest .01 percent of Americans have more than quintupled their share of the country's total wealth.

With the rise of the online economy from the 1990s onward, there was no reboot of the broken growth engine of US capitalism, as some enthusiasts expected. It did not, and could not, replace the much-diminished manufacturing sector, which had propelled decades of rapid economic expansion and relatively broadly shared prosperity before the bottom fell out in the 1970s. A privatized internet would not inaugurate a new golden era; rather, it would settle comfortably into the existing coordinates of a new gilded age. Its economic legacy would be the creation of islands of super-profits in a sea of stagnation, the minting of several dozen billionaires in a time of flat and falling wages, the hypertrophy of select real estate markets in the midst of widespread housing insecurity. For those who occupy or orbit these new zones of power, privatization is a success story. For those who don't, the picture is more complicated.

8

Inclusive Predators

Doug Schifter spent more than forty years driving for a living in New York City. Then, in 2011, Uber came to town. Over the next several years, the company flooded the city with ride-hail cars. Schifter's income as a black-car driver collapsed, even as he began working 120-hour weeks. He maxed out his credit cards, missed a mortgage payment, and started moving his things into storage. Finally, on the morning of February 5, 2018, he drove up to City Hall and killed himself with a shotgun.

He wanted his suicide to be a statement. He had spent years excoriating Uber and its political allies for destroying his livelihood in a regular column for the trade publication *Black Car News*. In a note he posted to Facebook shortly before his death, he described the dire situation created by gig companies. "Due to the huge numbers of cars available with desperate drivers trying to feed their families," he wrote, "they squeeze rates to below operating costs and force professionals like me out of business. They count their money and we are driven down into the streets we drive becoming homeless and hungry. I will not be a slave working for chump change. I would rather be dead."

We can never fully understand what transpires in the mind of someone who decides to take their own life. Still, according to Schifter's own account, Uber played a role. His story thus offers a window into the world the modern internet has helped create, and a lesson in the complexity—and, all too often, the cruelty—of its effects.

An Entangled Existence

As privatization ascended from the basement of the internet into its upper floors, from the pipes to the so-called platforms, it programmed the profit motive into the network. This introduced a certain sameness across the stack: the purpose of both Comcast and Facebook is to make money. But beneath this sameness is a great deal of variation: Comcast and Facebook make money in quite different ways. The social consequences are also quite different.

Comcast makes money by selling access to the internet. An accommodating regulatory regime, secured through decades of diligent lobbying, enables companies like Comcast to provision this access on maximally extractive terms. Investors are rewarded while infrastructure is neglected. The result is an acutely undemocratic arrangement. Poor and rural users have it the worst, but even those in better-connected areas often endure low speeds and spotty service. Connectivity, a precondition for the possibility of a self-determined life, is unevenly and precariously distributed. Meanwhile, communities of all kinds are denied the opportunity to participate in the decisions that affect them. These decisions are made by executives and shareholders, and are tightly delineated by the profit motive.

Up the stack, where the online mall was born and took root, the situation is somewhat different. Here money is made not from selling access but by monetizing activity. But there are many kinds of activities being monetized, and they are monetized in several distinct ways. If telecoms are in the business of putting packets through a tube, online malls are a more varied species. They are also more complicated.

Take Uber. Uber is an internet company. The internet furnishes the connective tissue that links the smartphone apps of its drivers with those of its riders, and both to its software in the cloud. But technology is only one element of Uber's success, and a smaller one than is often supposed. As the legal scholar Veena Dubal has argued, and as Doug Schifter observed in his columns, politics has been pivotal, in particular the pressure the company has brought to bear on regulators and policymakers. In city after city, this pressure has enabled Uber to evade long-standing municipal rules regarding fares and the number of vehicles allowed on the road. Equally important is the limitless supply of money provided by investors, which can be used to bankroll lobbying, as well as to subsidize the cheap fares that undercut existing livery drivers like Schifter. Finally, the legal classification of ride-hail drivers as independent contractors is a pillar of the business model, since it keeps labor costs low.

Each of these elements is inseparable from the internet. The fact that Uber is an internet company has helped it persuade politicians and regulators that it should be exempt from a century of taxi regulations—indeed, that it represents a novel corporate form, a "Transportation Network Company."

Similarly, Uber's large trove of data, manufactured through the internet, has helped convince investors to finance the firm so generously. And the managerial algorithms that this data nourishes have helped maintain the fiction that drivers are independent contractors, as bossing people around through an app camouflages the reality of Uber's rule.

These interactions illustrate an important point. An online mall is an assemblage of technical components, but the components are entangled with a wider set of political, legal, and financial forces. These entanglements are functional—they are what makes the online mall work. They are not a context so much as a medium, not a backdrop against which the online mall operates but the channels that it operates through.

An online mall never exists in its "pure" form. It carries certain signatures—it is a middleman, a sovereign, and a beneficiary of network effects—and it is invariably devoted to the manufacture and monetization of data. But these characteristics are always expressed through the distinct institutional mesh in which a particular online mall is embedded—that is, through its entanglements. This explains how Google and Facebook and Amazon and Uber can share basic features while differing in their downstream effects. All are designed to make money from the upper floors of the internet. But the consequences of this pursuit, the imprints it leaves on the world, are fairly diverse.

Even so, a common theme can be detected. Online malls, whatever their particular entanglements, are inequality machines. More specifically, they reallocate the existing distribution of risk and reward. They push risks downward and spread them around. They pull rewards upward and focus them in fewer hands.

Risk and Reward

In his suicide note, Doug Schifter reflected on life before Uber. Taxi regulations "limited competition so in bad times everyone still made a good living," he recalled. Those regulations, won by drivers through collective action a century earlier, were risk-reduction techniques. By limiting the supply of taxis, they reduced the risk that drivers wouldn't pick up enough fares to earn an adequate living.

Uber's arrival changed that. "Now there are too many feeding off the same pie and there is not enough for everyone," wrote Schifter. It became harder to get fares. And, because both livery and ride-hail drivers are generally considered independent contractors—the model was widespread in the taxi industry before Uber—there was no regular wage to fall back on. Not everyone suffered, however. As drivers' livelihoods became more precarious, Uber's valuation rose. Its executives did well, its engineers did relatively well, and its investors did fabulously well.

The upshot, as Schifter predicted, was that a profession that once afforded its practitioners a reasonably lower-middle-class life became pauperized. Although the companies' close hold of the data makes precise national numbers impossible to obtain, a number of studies have shown that wages for ride-hail drivers in various urban markets are low. They typically earn less than the minimum wage and are often poor. A 2019 study by researchers at Georgetown University found that half of Uber drivers surveyed in Washington, DC, lived at or below the federal poverty line.

Inspired by Uber's example, a succession of startups have tried to "Uberize" other services. Their efforts have gathered fresh strength from the passage of Proposition 22 in California, a 2020 ballot measure that cemented the legal status of gig workers as independent contractors. This outcome was more or less purchased with a $200 million campaign conducted by gig companies, though at the time of writing the law's future is in doubt: in August 2021, a California judge ruled that the measure violated the state's constitution, prompting the gig companies to file an appeal. Regardless, the industry continues to pursue similar legislation in other states and at the national level. In an op-ed, venture capitalist Shawn Carolan declared that Proposition 22's example could open the way to Uberizing everything from agriculture to health care to software engineering. Employers are also feeling emboldened: a month after Proposition 22's success, the supermarket chain Albertsons replaced hundreds of unionized delivery employees in California with DoorDash drivers. The scenario is one that Schifter himself foresaw. "It is too late for me so who is next?" he wrote in his final Facebook post. "Maybe you and yours?"

For every worker in front of an app, however, there are many more standing behind it. Indeed, online malls of all kinds are labor-intensive. Only a portion of this labor is performed by direct employees. Much of it is performed by the subcontracted members of a vast shadow workforce, who do everything from cook food for the marvelous lunches served in elite Silicon Valley offices to operate the data centers on which the cloud depends.

They also perform the repetitive tasks that keep the machinery of online malls running, from labeling training datasets for machine learning models to scrubbing social media sites of obscene or offensive content. This latter layer is what anthropologist Mary L. Gray and computer scientist Siddharth Suri call "ghost work," and it is especially large and especially global. From Kenya to India to the United States, workers are hunched over monitors, being timed on how quickly they flag a "dick pic" or classify a photo of a dog. They are the human automata that automated systems, or systems that appear to be automated, are built on.

This shadow workforce is just as indispensable to the smooth operation of online malls as the relatively small number of direct employees who write the code and design the user interfaces. Yet shadow workers typically earn much lower pay and receive fewer to no benefits, despite working for some of the most profitable companies in the world. Sometimes, as in the case of social media content moderators who spend all day sifting through imagery of beheadings and child abuse, they also face traumatizing working conditions. They are made to bear the risks, while the rewards flow elsewhere.

There's nothing unique about tech's outsourcing of labor, of course—in the era of the fissured workplace, it's the norm. What's distinct about online malls is the particular way in which risk and reward tend to be redistributed: through a process called "predatory inclusion."

Predatory inclusion, argues the sociologist Tressie McMillan Cottom, is one of the dynamics that define the political economy of the internet. She describes it as "the logic, organization, and technique of including marginalized consumer-citizens into ostensibly democratizing mobility schemes on extractive terms." What does this mean in practice? Cottom gives the example of online colleges. Online colleges are disproportionately attended by Black women, who take on large student loans they often struggle to pay off. The inclusion of a historically excluded group is achieved, but on predatory terms.

This is a common pattern within online malls. Black and brown Americans who come from communities with persistently high rates of unemployment can make money as gig workers. Women kept at home by caregiving responsibilities can make money doing digital piecework while the baby sleeps. Slum dwellers in poor countries can make money labeling datasets. And so on: people whose lives and labor have been devalued through the historical and ongoing exclusions of racism, sexism, and imperialism can find a toehold in the elastic workplaces of the internet.

The internet, by enabling firms to distribute work while retaining control over the distributed workers, has helped absorb more layers of humanity into the wage relation. But this is accomplished in such a way that reinscribes the prior exclusions. The livelihoods on offer are meager and menial, not to mention highly insecure. The excluded are included, but only on the condition that they absorb most of the risk and forfeit most of the reward.

Remastered

Predatory inclusion isn't limited to the world of work. It is a broader phenomenon, with broader effects. It also shapes the media environments created by online malls, those privately owned public spaces where people acquire information, congregate, and socialize.

On a spring morning in 2011, a doctoral student named Safiya Umoja Noble typed "black girls" into Google and hit enter. The results surprised her. She was looking for activities for her young stepdaughter. What Google gave her was porn sites. "This best information, as listed by rank in the search results, was certainly not the best information for me or for the children I love," she later recalled. "For whom, then, was this the best information, and who decides?" This question set in motion the research project that would form the basis for Noble's dissertation and, later, her first book.

In the 1990s, the idea of cyberspace as a realm beyond race and gender was everywhere. Television commercials of the time trafficked in it; so did prominent pundits. Bodies would be left behind, along with the differences that marked them and the injustices that attended those differences. "Ours is a world that is both everywhere and nowhere," wrote the cyber-libertarian John Perry Barlow in 1996, "but it is not where bodies live."

Yet it was abundantly clear that the internet was indeed a place where bodies lived, though this clarity was mostly reserved for those who inhabited bodies that were not white and not male. Cyberspace was suffused with the bigotries that users brought with them. "It wasn't a question about if and when racism would rear its ugly head in this new world," explains Charlton McIlwain in his history of the Black internet. "Racism, fueled by anti-blackness, was already there when it began." One didn't have to spend much time in the message forums and chat rooms of the early internet to encounter racism and misogyny. Organized hate groups also built a beachhead: the neo-Nazi David Duke was an enthusiastic early adopter, praising the internet as a tool for "racial enlightenment."

The fact that oppression appeared in online spaces didn't mean it appeared in exactly the same form. The boundary between online and off was porous, but a boundary nevertheless. A new medium demanded new modulations. The scholar Lisa Nakamura, who began studying the phenomenon in the 1990s, coined a term to describe what she saw: "cybertyping." "Images of race from older media are the analog signal that the Internet optimizes for digital reproduction and transmission," she writes. To turn a vinyl record into a CD, you have to convert an analog signal into a digital one. Similarly, cybertyping involved the remastering of oppression for the internet—a process that "preserves the 'content' of the original piece while optimizing it for a new format."

But the internet would change significantly over the years. As the artisanal network of the 1990s gave way to the machines and monopolies of the new millennium, as the online malls began to centralize and standardize online life, oppression would be remastered once again. Turning a vinyl record into a CD changes the format, but at least it preserves the concept of the album. Compare this with streaming services like Spotify, where the album has been eclipsed by the algorithmically generated playlist. Something analogous happened with cybertyping as privatization moved up the stack and the internet entered the era of the online mall. Oppression became not only digital, not only networked, but algorithmic.

This is why Safiya Umoja Noble decided to call her book *Algorithms of Oppression*. Information in the early internet was mostly organized by humans; information in the era of the online mall is mostly organized by algorithms. Automation was central to Google's value proposition from the start: since its dorm-room days at Stanford, the search engine promised a programmatic way to measure the quality and relevance of websites, rather than relying on human moderators as Yahoo!

did. As Google moved off-campus and became a business, the economic advantage of this approach became clear. Human moderators were expensive; Google would let the algorithms do the work.

At first, the algorithms were fairly straightforward. But over the years, they have become byzantine beyond description. How Google ranks websites is the product of an immensely complex computation operating on many different inputs—so complex that even Google engineers have trouble explaining certain results. Moreover, the code is a closely guarded trade secret, so outsiders can have no knowledge of the exact mechanisms. Still, the broad outlines are known.

The search engine examines the contents of websites and the relationships among them, while a set of feedback loops enables the system to "learn" from the behavior of those who use it. Meanwhile, the owners of websites tweak their code to make them more appealing to the algorithms. This is called "search engine optimization" (SEO), and it can help websites climb the ladder into the coveted first page of results. Finally, advertisers can purchase ads associated with certain search terms. The interaction of these activities is what caused Google to return porn sites when Noble searched for "black girls" in 2011. It no longer does—the algorithms are frequently updated, causing search rankings to shift. Yet, as Noble notes, it's easy to find other instances of biased results: a Google Images search for "unprofessional hairstyles for work" continued to show mostly Black women with natural hair, for example.

This is what cybertyping looks like in the age of the online mall. And it follows a familiar logic: the logic of predatory inclusion. On the one hand, Google appears to offer a richer informational milieu than print, television, or film. You can search for nearly any subject and find websites related to it. This means that groups that have traditionally been under-represented in media can be amply, even abundantly represented. Yet this greater inclusivity is often achieved in such a way that reiterates the original exclusions. Black women might be more visible in a Google search, but this increased visibility is filtered through stereotypes that have long circulated in older media, such as the perception of Black women as hypersexual and unprofessional.

Ideologies like racism are not perpetuated by stereotypes alone. They "must be constantly created and verified in social life," explains the historian Barbara J. Fields. They must be sustained through collective practices, policy choices, and institutional arrangements that generate group-differentiated outcomes like higher rates of poverty and incarceration among Black Americans. Here too online malls are implicated. For years, Facebook let advertisers target users on the basis of race, gender, disability, and other traits. This kind of discrimination is forbidden under federal law when it comes to ads for employment, housing, and credit. It wasn't until 2019, after being sued by the US Department of Housing and Urban Development and the ACLU, that Facebook finally over-hauled its ads portal.

But discrimination persists. Even if a lender can no longer say they want their mortgage ad to be shown only to white borrowers, they can still use proxies to find alternative routes to the same audience. For example, they can target by job title, and choose occupations that are mostly white, like soft-ware engineering. The algorithm itself also contributes to such exclusions. Facebook aims to show people more "relevant" ads, using historical data about how different users have inter-acted with different kinds of advertising. If Black women are less likely to click on mortgage lending ads, and Facebook's code has inferred from an analysis of your online activity that you are a Black woman, then you are less likely to see a mort-gage lending ad. When a team of researchers at Northeastern University, the University of Southern California, and the nonprofit Upturn ran a series of Facebook ads targeted to randomized audiences, they found widespread discrimination of this kind. Job postings for nurses were shown to more women; those for janitors, to more Black people. Certain groups are "seen" by software, but being seen only marks their members for unequal treatment by companies who capitalize on that inequality. As with other forms of predatory inclusion at work within online malls, reward is concentrated and risk is diffused.

Innovation Opportunists

In 2015, a neo-Nazi named Dylann Roof killed nine Black people at a church in downtown Charleston, South Carolina. According to a manifesto he posted online, Google played a part in his radicalization. As Safiya Umoja Noble describes, Roof did a search for "black on white crime," and came across a site run by the Council of Conservative Citizens, a white-nationalist hate group. Through the algorithmic mediations of Google's online mall, fascist propaganda found a receptive reader.

Roof's fateful encounter points to another meaning of predatory inclusion. Online malls are predatory not just in *how* they include but in *who* they include. The Council of

Conservative Citizens would've had trouble reaching a wide audience through traditional media. But they managed to grab a high-ranking spot in Google's search results, presumably through the use of SEO techniques. This kind of manipulation turns out to be quite common, especially in social media. And it is central to how online malls generate inequality.

Online malls are inequality machines in part because they offer new opportunities to political forces committed to promoting inequality. These are the forces of the Right, which, as the political scientist Corey Robin argues, has always been devoted to the defense of hierarchy. Yet this defense is a surprisingly radical one. Since modern conservatism first took shape in the aftermath of the French Revolution, it has waged insurgencies from above to combat insurgencies from below. The point is not the preservation of the ancien régime but its reconstitution on a reinvigorated basis, what Robin calls the "new old regime."

Seeing conservatives as radicals helps explain a theme found throughout their history: their remarkable creativity with the media technologies of their time. In every era, they are "innovation opportunists," to borrow a term from the sociologist Jessie Daniels. Direct mailing campaigns were central to their success in the 1970s, talk radio in the 1980s and 1990s. In our era, they have turned their talents to the internet, particularly social media. Through a well-organized offensive, right-wing activists have made social media into an accelerator for their politics. Indeed, the resurgence of the far Right, both in the US and around the world, is hard to imagine without this development. It was David Duke, former Ku Klux Klan grand wizard, and not John Perry Barlow, former

Grateful Dead lyricist, who saw the future of the internet most clearly.

But how has Duke's vision been fulfilled, exactly? How do the online malls of social media politicize people? This is a matter of much complexity, and much confusion.

Beyond the Bubble

The popular version goes something like this: users are being brainwashed by disinformation. Disinformation is promoting polarization. It is disseminated primarily by foreign agents. It is designed to elicit strong emotions like anger so that it can spread more easily. It spreads more easily because social media sites are optimized for user engagement—capturing more user attention means collecting more advertising dollars—and content that provokes and enrages naturally gets more engagement. Finally, algorithmically generated echo chambers—"filter bubbles"—create perfect vectors for such content. Insulated from the moderating influence of mainstream media, and from the dissenting views of other users, these bubbles become breeding grounds for extremism.

There are elements of truth to this story. But it is mostly misleading. It makes a number of questionable assumptions, and rests on an oversimplified, mechanistic model of how software and psychology and politics interact.

Polarization is a good place to start. The term is notoriously imprecise. Some researchers focus on "affective polarization"— basically, how much Republicans and Democrats hate each other—while others look at ideology, voting patterns, and other metrics. But however polarization is defined, there is little evidence that social media causes it. One study, done by the economists Levi Boxell, Matthew Gentzkow, and Jesse M. Shapiro, even found that polarization—defined here as a composite of eight measures, from how ideologically consistent someone's views are to how rarely they split their votes across the two parties—has "increased the most among the demographic groups least likely to use the Internet and social media," which is to say, people older than sixty-five.

The polarization frame has a further problem: it evokes a false equivalence between Left and Right. It is certainly true that left-wing movements have benefited from social media. Occupy Wall Street, Black Lives Matter, and the candidacies of Bernie Sanders probably wouldn't have reached the scale they did without Twitter and Facebook. The power shift from traditional media to the more distributed informational worlds of social media has created more room for social-democratic, socialist, and abolitionist ideas to circulate.

But the Right has immeasurably more resources with which to exploit this shift. They have deep-pocketed donors, a sophisticated media operation, and undiluted control of the Republican Party. It is no accident that the top-performing link posts from public Facebook pages in the US are mostly from right-wing pundits like Ben Shapiro.

What's more, it is figures like these, and not foreign government operatives, who are the main purveyors of false information on social media. Researchers at New York University found that far-right news sources receive the highest levels of engagement per follower, and that such sources are actually more popular if they spread false information—which is not the case for news sources in the political center or on the left. Meanwhile, despite the amount of attention devoted to the role of Russian influence operations in the 2016 election, they had no measurable effect, according to research by Yochai Benkler, Robert Faris, and Hal Roberts. Further, such operations "mostly took the form of jumping on the bandwagon" of the Right, Benkler writes, boosting false narratives initially manufactured by domestic forces.

These forces have a wide range of outlets at their disposal. They can circulate propaganda not just through social media but across an entire right-wing media ecosystem, from talk radio to cable TV to news sites. These different modes overlap and interpenetrate: Fox News is both the most-viewed US cable network and one of the most popular US publishers on Facebook. Right-wing groups are often quite successful at smuggling their narratives into centrist mainstream media as well, using a set of techniques that researchers Alice Marwick and Rebecca Lewis call "trading up the chain." Outlets well outside of the right-wing media ecosystem can be conscripted into promoting reactionary propaganda and even outright hoaxes.

Trading up the chain isn't just about amplification—it's also about legitimation. Getting more, and more popular, places to repeat something makes it seem more credible. In other words, persuasion is involved. This brings us to an essential point: the internet does not brainwash users because brainwashing is a myth. The information that people encounter online matters, but its relationship with their beliefs is nonlinear: Dylann Roof did not became a neo-Nazi on the basis of a single Google search. Human beings are complicated and contradictory. So is the process whereby they acquire their ideological frames.

This messiness is manifest in online spaces, contrary to the "filter bubbles" thesis—which, like the theory that polarization is produced by social media, has scant evidence to support it. People can and do find like-minded interlocutors on the internet, and the algorithms that underpin social media feeds and recommendation systems can contribute to these clusterings. But the conversations that ensue rarely resemble an echo chamber, with everyone parroting the same party line. When the researchers P. M. Krafft and Joan Donovan examined the origins of one campaign to spread false information on 4chan, a message board popular with the far Right, they found "widespread heterogeneity of beliefs and contestation of the claims." Even in a forum with a broadly shared ideology, people didn't blindly swallow a politically convenient lie. Instead, they argued. And it was precisely this skepticism, this surplus of views, that forced the partisans of the campaign to work harder. They couldn't count on their narrative to gain traction no matter what. So they had to develop "an arsenal of tactics" to circulate it more widely through social media, Krafft and Donovan explain.

What kind of tactics? Right-wing propagandists employ a variety of techniques. Just as "filter bubbles" can't be relied upon to reflexively amplify whatever falsehoods are fed to them, there is nothing automatic about how the algorithms of social media promote reactionary propaganda. It's not merely a matter of making one's content sufficiently outrageous— "rage-bait," as it's sometimes called—and letting Facebook do the rest.

This is not to deny that such content travels well. The digital enclosures of social media were built from the ground up to maximize user engagement. The more data that can be made about someone, the more "targeted" the ads can become; the longer that person spends on the site or app, the more ads can be served. Unsurprisingly, there appears to be a strong link between Facebook's insatiable appetite for eyeballs and the extent to which its filtering algorithms favor provocative content. Indeed, according to the journalist Karen Hao, research within Facebook itself has confirmed the existence of this link. Sensationalism sells, on social media as on other media.

But the code that determines what people see on Facebook, like the code that determines what they see in a Google search, is both complex and constantly changing. Indeed, in response to criticism, Facebook has experimented with prioritizing different kinds of engagement, and has employed various strategies—including putting resources toward building automated systems and hiring more content moderators—to ferret out content judged to be "toxic." Moreover, the mechanics of each social media mall are different: YouTube is one of the most important engines of right-wing radicalization on the internet, and reactionaries have developed an entire catalog of strategies specific to it. There is no single method the Right has used to master social media. The only constant among its propagandists is creativity.

Balancing Act

To say the truth is less tidy than commonly supposed does not absolve tech companies of responsibility. To say that algorithms and brains do not act as interlocking gears to form a single seamless apparatus of "polarization" does not mean that online malls are innocent. It means rather that we need better metaphors with which to clarify their complicity. This is where thinking in terms of entanglements can once again be useful.

The online malls of social media are collections of technical artifacts—algorithms, servers—that are entangled with collections of social artifacts—laws, markets, ideologies—through which they act on the world. One way to visualize the sum total of these relationships is, to follow a suggestion from the philosopher Félix Guattari, to see them ecologically. Ecosystems are full of feedback loops, cycles, and flows; organisms are ceaselessly interacting with one another and with the nonliving. Explaining how something happens within an ecosystem—the death and decomposition of an organism, say—requires examining the many interactions that have coincided to produce it. Something similar is required to explain how right-wing radicalization happens online. The internet is part of the answer, but only a part.

If the way in which social media companies contribute to the phenomenon is far from simple, however, the way in which they benefit from it is quite straightforward. Some interactions within an ecosystem are symbiotic—and symbiosis perfectly describes the dynamic between the Right and social media companies. The former gets a megaphone for their ideas; the latter gets lots of high-engagement users whose attention can be sold to advertisers.

While this relationship is mutually beneficial, it is not without its tensions. Occasionally embarrassments arise. A Facebook group called Stop the Steal was an excellent source of engagement until its members stormed the US Capitol in January 2021, prompting a crackdown from the company and an internal report that confirmed its role in the riot. Similarly, Facebook made a lot of money from the right-wing conspiracist movement QAnon until rising public pressure, particularly surrounding hoax-mongering by QAnon-linked accounts during the 2020 presidential election cycle, pushed the company to implement a half-hearted, and not particularly effective, ban.

These measures are motivated by profit considerations. When reactionaries go off the rails, advertisers can get nervous; as Facebook vice president of global affairs Nick Clegg explains, "Advertisers don't want their brands and products displayed next to extreme or hateful content." The incentive for social media companies is thus to accommodate right-wing propaganda networks, and their lucrative levels of engagement, right up to the point where their activities provoke sufficient public opprobrium, or sufficient violence, to alienate advertisers. This is a delicate balance to strike; indeed, Facebook never quite manages it.

Making the balancing act more delicate is pressure from the Republican Party. Republican politicians often accuse tech companies of censoring conservative views online. Given the visibility of the Right on social media, the accusation is clearly false, but it serves a useful purpose. By complaining about anti-conservative bias, Republicans can "work the ref" and bludgeon Facebook into being even more hospitable to right-wing propaganda. It's effective: Mark Zuckerberg has gone out of his way to curry favor with Republican leaders, and to mold Facebook's content policies to their liking. Joel Kaplan, a high-ranking Republican within Facebook who serves as the company's vice president of global public policy, wields particularly broad power. Kaplan has repeatedly intervened to promote the circulation of right-wing content on the site, and to push for content moderation rules and algorithm tweaks that favor the Right.

Again, these moves make good business sense. Facebook needs cordial relationships with Republicans in Congress and in statehouses across the country to maintain a favorable policy environment for profit-making. It spends a small fortune on lobbying for this very reason: forestalling regulatory shifts that might hurt its bottom line is a top priority. Still, Facebook can't afford to overinvest in Republicans at the expense of Democrats; after all, the latter also hold a fair bit of power. This makes the balancing act harder still.

Multiple Choice

The story of Facebook's complicated symbiosis with the Right holds a larger lesson about online malls. On the one hand, the inequalities they generate are inseparable from the pursuit of profit. The privatization of the upper floors of the internet is their basic prerequisite. But the profit motive does not always point in one direction. As the case of Facebook makes clear, sometimes what's best for the business isn't entirely obvious; there are competing motivations and constraints. In capitalism, the imperative to accumulate is absolute, but there is typically more than one way to satisfy this imperative.

The supremacy of the profit motive, then, does not alone determine the present shape of the internet. There are other privatized possibilities. And it is in these possibilities that a new wave of reformers, eager to mitigate a host of harms that have grown too large to ignore, place their hopes. They want to retain an internet controlled by private firms and run for profit, but they would like profit to be pursued in a less damaging way.

9

Toward the Forest

The soundtrack to the privatization of the internet was applause. The country's most powerful people expressed their enthusiasm at every step. In the 1990s, the takeover of the pipes by the telecoms enjoyed bipartisan backing. In the 2000s and into the 2010s, as the online malls were consolidating, a chorus of voices in high places cheered them on. In those days, tech was "the Teflon industry," in the words of journalist Rana Foroohar: widely celebrated by mainstream politicians and largely indulged by mainstream media. The notion that there might be negative consequences to its growing power was safely quarantined in academia, a few activist spaces, and the more adversarial edges of independent media.

At some point, however, the tone began to change. If a factory keeps polluting a river, people will eventually notice it's full of sludge, no matter how many newspaper columns they read about how beautiful the factory's widgets are. The 2016 presidential election proved to be the turning point in this respect. Facebook in particular became a prime target of criticism, driven by the (true) belief that it had hosted Russian influence operations and the (false) belief that such operations had been decisive in Trump's victory. This scandal supplied the initial spark; a long series of subsequent scandals fed the fire. While some involved new revelations—as journalists and politicians began, for the first time, investigating online malls in earnest—others centered on normal industry practices that were hiding in plain sight. What was once business as usual now became the basis of Capitol Hill hearings. The "techlash" had arrived.

As the years have passed, the techlash has persisted. Its imprint appears to be permanent. The spectacle of the tech industry behaving badly has become routine, even cliché—a spectacle ritually enacted in the periodic testimony of its executives before Congress. Meanwhile, polling suggests that public opinion has taken a turn: in 2019, only 50 percent of Americans said that tech companies have a positive effect on the United States, compared with 71 percent in 2015.

This doesn't mean that change is inevitable. Public opinion has no reliable relationship with public policy: plenty of ideas that are broadly popular, like single-payer health care, are nonstarters in a political system whose priorities are largely set by corporations and the rich. Nevertheless, internet reform has become something of a preoccupation in policymaking circles in recent years.

Internet reform is by no means monolithic: the particular proposals and points of emphasis vary widely. Still, it's possible to discern two tendencies—which are, in practice, often joined together. The first involves writing new rules about how companies are allowed to behave, or enforcing existing ones. Examples include the California Consumer Privacy Act, a state law enacted in 2018 that gives residents certain rights regarding the collection and processing of their personal data, or the ongoing efforts to hold Facebook accountable for violating federal law with its discriminatory ad delivery. (The Right, for its part, remains fixated on the idea that its speech is being censored online—a useful fiction for working the refs at Facebook and elsewhere, but one that fatally compromises the seriousness of its proposals.)

The second trend aims at reducing the market power of the big firms. This is the focus of the "New Brandeisians," a group of anti-monopoly advocates who have become influential within the Democratic Party and even among a number of Republicans. They take their inspiration from Louis Brandeis, a leading liberal jurist of the Progressive Era who believed monopolies posed a threat to democracy. His solution, taken up by his modern-day disciples, was a Madisonian system of checks and balances, designed to disperse corporate power and promote fair competition.

Toward this end, the New Brandeisians urge a range of measures for cracking down on tech monopolies. In some cases, they want to break large firms into smaller ones: one proposal calls for forcing Facebook to spin off WhatsApp, Instagram, and its ad network. In other cases, they are willing to accept a certain degree of bigness and to constrain such "natural monopolies" through regulation. Above all, they want to make markets more competitive. They believe that more competition will bring a number of benefits, from a wider distribution of wealth to reduced corporate influence over the political process.

Their advocacy is having a noticeable effect. In October 2020, the House Judiciary Committee concluded a sixteen-month investigation into Amazon, Apple, Google, and

Facebook with a strongly worded report that recommended various New Brandeisian reforms. The same month, the Department of Justice (DOJ) joined with eleven state attorneys general to file a major antitrust lawsuit against Google. By the summer of 2021, a legislative package of six bills designed to strengthen antitrust enforcement was working its way through the House. President Biden has been especially active on the issue, selecting the prominent New Brandeisian scholar Lina Khan to chair the FTC and the antitrust lawyer Jonathan Kanter to lead the DOJ's Antitrust Division, as well as issuing an executive order that directs more than a dozen federal agencies to pursue pro-competition initiatives. It remains to be seen how much of the anti-monopoly agenda will ultimately be implemented. Some congressional Republicans remain implacably opposed, while the judiciary presents obstacles of its own; when the FTC filed an antitrust suit against Facebook, a federal judge threw it out. But no matter what happens, a significant shift has already occurred. After years of letting the online malls do whatever they liked, politicians have finally become less forgiving.

Market Forces

Each strain of internet reform has its merits. The rule-makers are right that the online malls are too lightly regulated. Just because a service is mediated by the internet doesn't mean it should be exempt from labor law, civil rights law, and any number of other laws that tech companies have successfully short-circuited over the years. The New Brandeisians are right that rulemaking is insufficient without also transforming how the internet is owned. Further, they recognize that the current configuration of ownership is not the natural order of things, but rather a contingent affair, constructed through public policy. "There are no such things as market 'forces,'" writes Khan. Rather, political economy is made, and can thus be remade.

Yet the political economy preferred by the New Brandeisians isn't a particularly radical departure from the present. They still want an internet ruled by markets, albeit one where markets are competitive rather than concentrated. The pursuit of profit would remain the organizing principle, but profit would be pursued by smaller and more entrepreneurial firms. And they believe that such a restructuring would go a long way toward addressing the concerns raised by the techlash.

But would it? Nick Srnicek notes that more competition could very well make things worse. "After all, it's competition— not size—that demands more data, more attention, more engagement and more profits at all costs," he writes. In the case of social media, observes liberal commentator Ezra Klein, more competition could "lead to yet fiercer wars for our attention and data, which would incentivize yet more unethical modes of capturing it." Competitive pressure compels companies to seek any possible advantage. Indeed, the industry practices with the most destructive effects, such as the obsession with user engagement, were first developed by social media firms when they were comparatively leaner and hungrier and needed to grab market share as quickly as possible—they came out of competition, in other words. It was only once these firms matured into monopolies that they could afford to take a somewhat longer view. Facebook now spends hundreds of millions of dollars each year on content moderation. It does so for perfectly self-interested reasons—to soothe advertisers and to forestall public relations disasters—and its efforts clearly fall short. But it's hard to imagine that it would have money to spare on such mitigations if it were locked in a deathmatch with several competitors.

As an alternative to pro-competition reforms, Klein proposes regulations of various kinds, modeled on those around airline safety and prescription drugs. A New Brand-eisian might respond that corporate giants are adept at co-opting the regulatory process. Regulation can also reinforce existing concentrations of private power by introducing compliance costs that only large corporations can bear. Indeed, big tech firms have repeatedly called for more regulation in recent years—provided they get to decide how they're regulated.

Facing Reality

Fortunately, rulemaking and anti-monopoly, or some combination of the two, aren't the only choices available to us. There is another strategy: deprivatization.

Making markets more regulated or more competitive won't touch the deeper problem, which is the market itself. The online malls are engineered for profit-making, and profit-making is what makes them inequality machines. The exploitation of gig and ghost workers; the reinforcement of racism, sexism, and other oppressions; the amplification of right-wing propaganda—none of these diverse forms of social damage would exist if they weren't profitable. It's true that these damages can be softened somewhat, and that larger firms can soften them more easily than smaller ones. But here too the market sets limits: Facebook can only spend so much on content moderation before its shareholders revolt. More importantly, its addiction to engagement, and the symbiosis with the Right that this addiction has engendered, is the very basis of its business model—which creates the problems that content moderation is supposed to address. The comparison that comes to mind is the tragicomedy of coal companies embracing carbon capture: it would be easier to simply stop burning coal.

Online malls are not inequality machines purely on account of their effects, however. Even if, miraculously, they stopped generating these effects—this is a thought experiment, not an actual possibility—a fundamental inequality would remain. Corporations would still own the internet. Immensely consequential decisions would be left in the hands of executives and investors, and these decisions would in turn be bound by the mandates of the market. Most people would have no say in the matters that centrally affect their lives.

A privatized internet will always amount to the rule of the many by the few, and the rule of those few by an imperative that is hard-wired into capitalism: the imperative to accumulate. Mark Zuckerberg is probably the most powerful man online, thanks to a shareholder structure that preserves his control of Facebook. A social network of more than 2 billion users is more or less a personal dictatorship. But even Zuckerberg can't defy the imperative to accumulate; shareholders would punish him in the form of a falling stock price, and, if it got bad enough, competitors would put him out of business.

Deprivatization opens the door to a different kind of internet. Just as community networks are challenging the legacy of privatization down the stack, a similar approach can be applied up the stack. The internet reformers want to make online malls into more responsible stewards of our digital sphere. A more realistic response, if one hopes to reach the root of the problem, is to abolish them.

Birds in the Food Court

What comes after the online mall? When real malls die, birds build nests in the food court. Bushes and trees claim the floors and walls. The enclosure no longer really encloses: skylights shatter, doors hang open, the line between inside and outside breaks down. Some decades or centuries later, a forest appears.

We can imagine something similar happening to the online equivalents. What's important is the pluralism of this picture. Down the stack, the community network is the main character in the making of a democratic internet. Up the stack, it's not quite so straightforward. There is no main character. The greater diversity of forms one encounters at this altitude, the distinctness of the different online malls and their entanglements, requires a greater range of approaches. Further, these approaches can't be spelled out in quite as much detail. They still need to be discovered and developed; what the deprivatized version of this layer looks like is still largely unknown. As a result, there is somewhat less to say.

To have more to say, we need more experiments. The goal of these experiments shouldn't be a one-to-one replacement of each online mall with its deprivatized doppelganger. You can't simply clone Facebook, place it under public or cooperative ownership, and expect substantially different results. Online malls organize online life through a particular architecture, and that architecture makes certain choices for us. To make new choices—to create spaces where we can make those choices collectively—we need new architectures.

The most useful framework for thinking about this problem comes, perhaps counterintuitively, from the movement for police and prison abolition. It turns out that the thinker whose ideas are best suited for building a better internet is not Louis Brandeis but Angela Davis. For decades, Davis and other abolitionists have argued that police and prisons can't be reformed. Rather, they are so dehumanizing and so incriminated in the reproduction of race and class hierarchies that they must be eliminated altogether.

This position often invites the accusation that abolitionists are hopelessly utopian. In fact, they are everywhere involved in daily politics. They have waged successful campaigns across the country to stop the construction of new prisons, to reduce incarcerated populations, and to defund the police. But, as Davis explains, "abolition is not primarily a negative strategy." It's also about "building anew." Abolitionists are not just trying to decrease the number of cops and prisons until both disappear. They are also coming up with better ways of keeping people safe.

To do so, Davis argues, it's essential to "let go of the desire to discover one single alternative system of punishment." The point is not to replace prisons with pseudo-prisons, or police with pseudo-police, but to assemble a "constellation of alternative strategies and institutions" that obviate the need for prisons and police: restorative justice programs, mental health services, community reinvestment, and demilitarized schools, among many others. These initiatives are interconnected; together they form a fabric that can "lay claim to the space now occupied" by the institutions that abolitionists are working to eradicate.

Davis and her abolitionist colleagues give us the basic blue-print for deprivatizing the upper floors of the internet. On the one hand, we can work to erode the power of the online malls. The anti-monopoly toolkit—breaking up tech giants, banning mergers and acquisitions, and other New Brandeisian methods—is valuable here. On the other hand, we can create a constellation of alternatives that, to use Davis's phrase, "lay claim to the space" that online malls currently occupy. The former tactic is designed to open cracks in the enclosures. The latter tactic aims at seeding those cracks with all manner of invasive species.

What might some of these species look like? A key aboli-tionist insight is that failures of imagination produce practical failures. The failure to imagine a world beyond prisons and police condemns reformers to keep reiterating old injustices in new forms. Indeed, as abolitionist organizer Sarah T. Hamid argues, reformism is a "carceral tactic"—it is a "means by which these systems have expanded over time." Electroni-cally monitored house arrest extends the prison into the home. Body cameras make police surveillance even more ubiquitous.

Protocolize the Walled Gardens

Abolishing the online malls requires, above all, imagination. Not imagination in the singular but in the plural: imagina-tion as an embodied, collective process of experimentation. This demands looking at technology differently. We must move away from "technology as an outcome to toolmaking as a practice," in the words of sociologist Ruha Benjamin. Tech-nology ceases to be something that is done *to* people, and becomes something they do together.

Programmers and artists and academics are already doing the imaginative work of envisioning an internet beyond the online malls. They are theorizing, and actively building, digital spaces where profit is not the priority and where users govern themselves. It is to their ideas and innovations that we can turn for a first draft of the path forward.

Instead of Facebook, imagine millions of social media communities, each with their own rules and customs and cultures. This is the vision of media scholar Ethan Zuckerman. These communities would be "plural in purpose": they would host different kinds of interactions. "Pool halls, libraries, and churches are all public spaces, but they all have different purposes, norms, and affordances," Zuckerman notes. There is no reason our online spaces can't have the same diversity.

The logic of the online mall is to enclose everything and get as big as possible. This bigness serves the interests of investors: it helps satisfy their appetite for outsize returns. More users mean more rents, more data, more profits. Plus, it brings the benefits of network effects, which neutralizes the competition and enhances the value of the firm.

But bigness "makes true participatory governance difficult, if not impossible," argues Zuckerman. "A 'community' of a billion people who have nothing in common but their use of a media platform is not a community in any meaningful sense." This brings us to another virtue of decentralization: not only does it facilitate greater diversity, it also enables a degree of democracy. At a small enough scale, social media communities can become self-governing. Instead of letting tech executives decide how filtering algorithms work or how content is moderated—behind closed doors and bound by the market—users can make their own choices, and those choices can be guided by considerations other than profit.

Just because such communities are small doesn't mean they have to be isolated. Decentralization is not the same as fragmentation. The internet is composed of distinct networks, but data travels easily across them because the networks share a common set of protocols. These protocols are open and nonproprietary: any network can join the internet so long as it follows the specified rules.

Mastodon is an open-source software project that applies this principle to social media. Servers are independently run but interconnect through open protocols to form a federation. They can also talk to non-Mastodon servers within a broader ensemble of federations—the "Fediverse"—so long as those servers also use the same protocols. Mastodon resembles Twitter, but the Fediverse offers a range of other services, including those modeled after YouTube, Facebook, and Instagram. Interoperability means that the advantages of network effects can be preserved without the network being owned by a single entity.

Email—the internet's original social application—works the same way. Gmail and Yahoo Mail are distinct services with distinct features. But users can still exchange messages, thanks to shared protocols. The fact that these protocols are open and nonproprietary is a direct consequence of the internet's public origins. Privatization has pushed things in the opposite direction: online life increasingly takes place within monolithic enclosures where interactions are governed by secret and proprietary algorithms. "Protocolizing" social media would break the walls of these walled gardens, and turn them inside out.

Public Programming

Mastodon is not tiny. It has millions of users, and it's far from the only experiment of its kind: a number of similar projects are being pursued across the "decentralized web" community. Still, these alternatives remain relatively niche in comparison to the offerings of the tech giants. Making them more robust, and more of a threat, will require public investment. Two institutions in particular offer ideal vehicles for such investment: public libraries and public media.

The United States has more than nine thousand public libraries. What if each one "had a federated social media server, and anybody with a library card could have an account?" asks the programmer Darius Kazemi. Piggybacking on existing public infrastructure is an excellent way to make new online spaces more accessible, and fasten them to a funding source. Using local libraries also adds a measure of accountability. "If your administrator is an employee of your local library, then there's a door you can go knock on," says Kazemi. "I can't go knock on Mark Zuckerberg's door and complain about something, but I can do that at the local library."

Libraries have a further advantage: they are full of librarians. Librarians are the original information workers. They retrieve, classify, curate, and contextualize information, and they do so not for profit, but as a public service. This is a service that is sorely needed in online spaces. As Safiya Umoja Noble notes, it is significant that funding for public libraries has fallen as Google and Facebook have grown. We have outsourced "our knowledge needs" to the online malls, which satisfy those needs according to commercial imperatives that inevitably compromise the quality of the knowledge provided.

Librarians are the ideal antidote. Joan Donovan has called for ten thousand librarians to be put to work "building systems for curating timely, local, relevant, and accurate information across social media platforms."

The problems that librarians help solve are not new. For-profit social media suffers from the same deficits in information quality as other kinds of for-profit media, and for the same reasons. "Profit motives drive commercial media to entertain, sell advertising, satisfy shareholders, and make as much money as possible," writes Victor Pickard, and these compulsions cut against the ethic of journalism as a public service, which "aspires to inform, enlighten, keep a check on the powerful, and provide a forum for diverse views and voices." This ethic has always been relatively weak within the highly commercialized US media sphere; media deregulation in the 1980s and 1990s weakened it further. The chief beneficiary is the Right, whose propagandists have mastered the art of "disinfotainment," from Rush Limbaugh to Fox News. More recently, the collapse of local newspapers has given them new opportunities, as donor-subsidized right-wing sites fill the void left by growing "news deserts."

Commercial media's failings have inspired generations of reformers and radicals to champion a different paradigm: public media. Just as the market can't guarantee people housing, health care, and the rest of life's necessities, neither can it guarantee access to reliable information. This is why Pickard wants a federally funded "permanent trust for public media" that would subsidize local news organizations across the country. He also suggests turning public libraries and post offices into "community media centers" that could help make local residents into local reporters.

Much of what circulates within social media channels is not user-generated but articles, videos, and podcasts from publishers of various kinds. Creating a public option for media production would ensure a better supply of content, and hopefully help crowd out right-wing propaganda. Pickard cites a body of academic research showing that public media tends to "present a wider range of voices and perspectives," and be "more critical of dominant policy positions." These strengths would do much to enhance the quality of information circulating within social media communities, particularly if the latter developed formal relationships with public media enterprises and local community media centers.

Another way to think of these interventions is as investments in care. The scholar Lindsay Bartkowski argues that content moderation is best understood as a form of care work and, like other forms of care work, is systematically undervalued. Certain kinds of caring go entirely unpaid—mothers bearing and raising children, for instance—while others are performed for menial pay, as in the case of the home health aides and nursing home staff who care for the elderly. Similarly, content moderation is typically a low-wage job, despite being as essential to the reproduction of our online social worlds as other kinds of care are to the reproduction of our offline social worlds. There is also a racial aspect: tech companies source much of their content moderation workforce from countries like the Philippines and India, following a broader pattern in which waged care workers tend to be Black, brown, or from the Global South. As Bartkowski writes, "Racialized workers are emotionally exploited, poorly compensated, and relegated to the 'underside' of the internet in order to support the production of a pseudo-domestic sphere that users of the

Global North virtually inhabit." Any project to improve social media must make such workers more valued and more visible, and enable them to form what Bartkowski calls "affinities and solidarities" with the users whose communities they care for.

A social media that is decentralized, self-governing, well cared for, anchored in public libraries, and enriched by public media won't be perfect, of course. Challenges will remain. For one, there will still be Nazis on the internet. This is a problem that cannot be solved online because it is not primarily an online problem. Still, a decentralized social media would be better designed to mitigate it. When the fascist social networking site Gab migrated to Mastodon, most of the servers that make up the Fediverse responded by blocking Gab. Because Mastodon is open-source, fascists are free to use it, but their communities can be quarantined. Decentralized social media moves "decision making out to the ends of the network, rather than keeping it centralized among a small group of very powerful companies," explains writer Mike Masnick. Some ends of the network may be populated by toxic elements. But with no single set of algorithms and executives to manipulate and intimidate, at least they can be denied a wider hearing.

Common Sense

Social media is only one genre of online mall. To abolish the rest, more imagination is needed. Nick Srnicek imagines a publicly owned cloud service that "ensures privacy, security, energy efficiency and equal access for all." Such a service might be carved out of a corporate provider like Amazon Web Services, which could be required to donate a portion of its capacity. Picture a "public lane" for the cloud, serving the digital infrastructure needs of a growing deprivatized sector.

This sector would include a variety of cooperative ventures, not just in social media but across all realms of online life. Here too experiments are plentiful and ongoing, particularly when it comes to creating worker-owned substitutes for gig economy firms. Up & Go is a group of home cleaning cooperatives in New York City that book appointments through their own app. These worker-owners earn more than the industry average, and have far more control over the conditions of their work. As Up & Go co-owner Marve Romero puts it, "Cooperativism is a different world."

Similar efforts exist around the globe, part of an active international community devoted to "platform cooperativism." Such efforts need public support. Fortunately, there are many policy instruments available, such as grants, loans, contracts, and preferential tax treatment. One could also imagine municipal regulatory codes that only allow app-based services to be performed by worker-owned firms, as the writer Seth Ackerman suggests. In normal times, politicians and regulators aren't likely to antagonize business interests. But sometimes tensions arise, and opportunities reveal themselves. In the fall of 2017, London's transportation agency announced it would not renew Uber's license to operate, citing a number of regulatory violations. In response, a left-wing think tank called the New Economics Foundation called for the mayor to create a cooperatively owned app-based taxi service to replace Uber. It didn't materialize, and Uber eventually returned to London. But the basic strategy is sound: bureaucratic exasperation with poorly behaved tech firms isn't going anywhere, and could possibly be leveraged into securing state backing for alternatives.

Then there is the question of data. Given the fact that online malls are organized around the manufacture and monetization of data, a deprivatized sector will need to find methods for dealing with it. To be effective, these methods must follow legal scholar Salomé Viljoen's admonition to look beyond the common tendency to see data production in personal terms and recognize its collective character. The data practices of a company like Facebook involve routine violations of individuals' privacy, but Facebook does not care about individuals—or rather, it only cares about individuals insofar as they represent, en masse, a source of "population-level insights" that can be used to sell ads. User behavior is analyzed in order to sort people into groups that make them legible to advertisers. This analysis can't happen at the level of a single individual: your information isn't particularly useful until it's combined with lots of other people's information.

Data is made collectively, and made valuable collectively. It follows that its governance should also be collective: that users should have the power "to shape the purposes and conditions of data production," in Viljoen's words. Toward that end, a number of proposals have been developed for "data trusts" and "data commons" of different kinds. The writer Evan Malmgren recommends a cooperatively owned data trust that grants voting shares to its members, who in turn elect a leadership that is empowered to negotiate over the terms of data use with other entities.

Crucially, the ownership of data would be separated from its processing: users could determine under what conditions an online service would have access to their data, and under what conditions more data could be manufactured. If people were given the chance to make their own decisions about how data is made and used, it's reasonable to expect they might make different decisions than those made by Mark Zuckerberg and friends. For instance, they might choose to ban the sort of sweeping surveillance that is so integral to online advertising. This architecture is also well suited to a more decentralized internet, since users could put their data in a central depot and then authorize use by different services—a cooperative social media server, a worker-owned delivery app—as needed.

Innovation from Below

These sketches are a good start, but they still bear the stamp of the internet they are trying to escape. The aspiration to create a decentralized Twitter or a worker-run Uber is a step in the right direction, but it remains imprisoned within an enemy paradigm. It suffers from a failure of imagination. And if we take seriously the abolitionist insight that failures of imagination produce practical failures, then abolishing the online malls is infeasible without a lot more creativity.

Creativity is a social act. Its inspirations are collective—they emanate from a milieu, a scene, a culture—even if the fashioning of this raw material into a finished work can sometimes be solitary. Currently, the creativity of the communities that are doing the best work reimagining the upper floors of the internet—under the banner of the "decentralized web," "platform cooperativism," or some other creed—is constrained by their narrow social base. They tend to attract specific kinds of people, generally those with technical skills and ample free time. Elevating the level of creativity involves making such spaces larger, more representative, and more integrated into everyday life.

An interesting model for doing so comes from 1980s London. In 1981, the left wing of the Labour Party won control of the Greater London Council (GLC), a municipal administrative body, and embarked on an ambitious economic program. At the time, London had high unemployment, in large part due to deindustrialization. The GLC responded by investing public money in unionized firms, as well as encouraging the creation of worker-owned cooperatives.

It also established five "Technology Networks" in different locations across the city. These were prototyping workshops, similar to "makerspaces" or "hackerspaces" today. People could walk in, get access to machine tools, receive training and technical assistance, and build things. The designs for the things they built went into a shared "product bank" that other people could draw from, and which were licensed for a fee to for-profit firms to help finance the Networks. The innovations that emerged included wind turbines, disability devices, children's toys, and electric bikes. Energy efficiency was an area of special emphasis. The Networks themselves were governed by a mix of local residents, trade unionists, tenant organizers, and academics.

One purpose of these spaces was to democratize the design and development of technology. This meant creating a participatory process whereby working-class communities could obtain the tools and the expertise they needed to make their own technologies. It meant producing to satisfy human need—what organizers at the time called "socially useful production"—rather than to maximize profit.

Satisfying human need necessitated the direct involvement of the particular humans whose needs were to be satisfied, since they were the ones who knew their needs best. As Network member Mary Moore explained, the goal was "making sure that what you do is going to be of real use to the intended users," which required "getting them to take part in the design process rather than just pop in with a product when you've produced it."

Sadly, the Networks were short-lived. Margaret Thatcher eliminated the GLC in 1986, and the Networks lost most of their funding. Those that managed to survive were forced to become more commercial, such as by offering job training services that businesses found useful; the radical elements fell away. This speaks to a central difficulty: the public sector can provide some cushioning from market pressures to make space for alternatives. But if those alternatives can't root themselves in such a way that enables them to become autonomous, and responsible for their own reproduction, they won't endure.

Even so, the London experience provides a valuable precedent. The Technology Networks are useful for thinking about how to abolish the online malls. It's conceivable that municipalities could create something like the Networks today, places where large numbers of people could contribute to the imaginative work of remaking the upper floors of the internet. They could team up with designers and developers to build alternative online services. Some might be hyperlocal; others might become regional, national, or even international. Some might be informal and volunteer-run; others might be placed under public ownership, or serve as the basis for new cooperatives.

For such efforts to be successful, they must blur the line between technology's creators and its users, and eventually aspire to make the two categories indistinguishable. Expertise would no longer be defined in an exclusively technical sense: some people are experts in programming, others in design, still others in their daily lives. "We believe that everyone is an expert based on their own lived experience, and that we all have unique and brilliant contributions to bring to a design process," state the principles of the Design Justice Network, an organization committed to developing more democratic design practices. An internet ruled by the people is one where people directly participate in the making of the internet. The scholar Sasha Costanza-Chock, a leading theorist of "design justice," cites the famous slogan of the disability rights movement: "Nothing about us without us."

Everything Else

Ideally, the latter-day Technology Networks would not only incubate new additions to the deprivatized sector but also embed them within a set of institutional relationships that keep them alive. Writing new software is relatively easy; creating sustainable and scalable alternatives to the online malls is the hard part. The "community wealth building" strategy for promoting community networks down the stack can be helpful here. Public and quasi-public anchor institutions like government agencies, hospitals, and universities could be mined for procurement contracts that funnel revenue to the deprivatized sector and help it grow. Cooperatives could form federations to collaborate with one another in various ways. Governments could encourage them with loans and grants and tax breaks.

But the biggest threat to the survival of the deprivatized sector will come from the tech companies themselves. Just as the telecoms have mounted a well-funded campaign to destroy community networks, we can expect a comparable corporate onslaught if the dominance of online malls were ever at risk. Better, then, to go on the offensive from the start.

One way to do so is technical. The writer Cory Doctorow talks about "adversarial interoperability," which describes a situation where one service communicates with another without the latter's permission, or perhaps only with grudging permission secured through legislation. For example, Facebook could be made to adopt open protocols that enable other social media applications to interconnect. Interoperability has become a central concern among the New Brandeisian anti-monopolists and across their wide sphere of influence, and has even begun to inspire some proposed legislation. Taken to its limit, interoperability could threaten the business model of online malls. If people could make their own ad-free applications for accessing Facebook content and communicating with Facebook users without using Facebook's site and apps, the company would lose advertising revenue. If Facebook users and the users of decentralized alternatives like Mastodon could easily interact, those alternatives might become more appealing to more people. Facebook would shrink, and perhaps even collapse.

But going on the offensive is more a political matter than a technical one. Here too the Technology Networks of 1980s London can offer inspiration. They weren't just places where people built things. They were also organizing spaces. The act of prototyping products in a workshop could serve as a starting point for a broader conversation about what kinds of transformations would be needed to create a more equitable society. In the process of trying to solve their problems with technology, people came to realize that technology often fell short of solving their problems. Politics was needed. Along these lines, one of the Networks kick-started a campaign called "Right to Warmth" that involved organizing community energy efficiency initiatives, creating local energy cooperatives, and pressuring Margaret Thatcher's government into putting more money toward energy conservation measures.

What kind of campaigns might materialize today? If online malls are defined by their entanglements, then they can't be dismantled without also unraveling the social phenomena they are entangled with. This might take the form of building unions among app-based workers, or reversing the runaway financialization that has underwritten the rise of the tech giants. It might mean working to weaken the material foundations of the Right. There are many possibilities, but one thing is clear: to remake the internet, we will have to remake everything else.

Conclusion

Future Nostalgia

On the early internet, there was a running joke: the internet was about to die. Not literally but spiritually: "imminent death of the net predicted!" as the joke became known. It poked fun at the grumblers who popped up every week or month or year on mailing lists or message boards to announce that the internet was about to lose whatever qualities had made it a good place to gather. They were easy to ridicule, but they had a point: the internet was always changing, even in the years before privatization. And these changes naturally stirred nostalgia in the hearts of users who had grown attached to a particular way of being online.

The nostalgics are no less numerous today. Their main object of mourning is the "open web": online life before it got enclosed by online malls. In those days, the story goes, the internet was freer, more creative. It revolved around open protocols, not proprietary algorithms, and no single site or company was too dominant. It had a "culture of serendipitous tinkering," says internet scholar Jonathan Zittrain. It resembled a gritty, eccentric metropolis, says cultural critic Virginia Heffernan. These are the characteristics being killed by the corralling of the internet into walled gardens—what Heffernan describes as "suburbanization."

Nostalgia never paints a reliable picture of the past. In this case, however, the past isn't even past. A hundred eulogies later, the open web lives on: the online malls haven't destroyed it so much as hijacked it. Openness is what lets companies like Google and Facebook sprinkle their software throughout the web—crawlers, trackers, ads—to siphon data back to their servers. Interoperability has been weaponized into *intra*operability, argues the scholar Anja Bechmann, serving an "asymmetrical power relationship" that privileges a few "data hubs and passage points." This is obviously a different arrangement than the one that prevailed before. But it's not quite accurate to say that the web was once open and now is closed—rather, it is the open parts of the web that make the closed parts possible.

As for whether the result is more "suburban"—boring— this claim is equally hard to sustain. Online malls are fascinating places. They are places where people make culture, do politics, launch movements, forge identities, cohere communities. Black Twitter, as the work of scholar André Brock, Jr. has shown, is one of the richest cultural repositories on the internet. Nostalgia for an internet before all this is also nostalgia for a time when fewer people used the internet, and when its users tended to be whiter and more affluent—an internet that was, for these reasons, much less interesting.

But nostalgia isn't supposed to be accurate. That's not why it sticks. It sticks because it expresses a feeling of loss that is sincerely felt, and this feeling has a reality all its own. At some point, everybody loses the internet they love: the internet of Gopher and Usenet, of Yahoo! and GeoCities, of Friendster and MySpace. Alongside these personal losses, however, is a collective loss: a series of missed opportunities to reimagine the internet. If internet nostalgia is inevitable, perhaps it can be linked to this larger loss, a loss that touches all of us, whether we realize it or not. And perhaps there is a political potential here that can be harvested for a higher end.

In his history of the English working class, the historian E. P. Thompson describes the political power of nostalgia, something that the Luddites, those machine-breakers of the nineteenth century, put to good use. The Luddites are best remembered today as a group of textile workers who destroyed the machinery that was throwing them out of work. But they were also thinkers, and they circulated their thoughts in poems, proclamations, petitions, songs, and letters. On the one hand, they lamented the disintegration of their social world under the advancing hurricane of industrial capitalism. On the other hand, they sketched an image of a new society, one in which "industrial growth should be regulated according to ethical priorities and the pursuit of profit be subordinated to human needs," writes Thompson. These two moves were connected: as Thompson explains, the Luddites looked backward *in order to* look forward. They used ancient values in order to invent a different modernity. In their imagined past, they discovered materials with which to imagine a future.

A social movement to remake the internet might follow a similar path. Maybe we can mourn the possible futures the internet might have had—futures that privatization, by programming the profit motive into every layer of the network, foreclosed. And maybe this nostalgia can help inspire the movement that will be needed to pry open a horizon shrunk by privatization and recover a wider field of view.

Movements are made of both creativity and coercion. Masses of people in motion generate new ideas, as the Luddites did. But they must also threaten enough disruption to have their ideas taken seriously. While movements don't always succeed—more often they don't—this dual character is the source of their strength: the combination of the capacity to envision a different future with the force necessary to achieve it. The absence of these two elements is what enabled privatization to proceed in the 1990s, 2000s, and 2010s, creating the internet we know today.

Understanding how privatization made the modern internet is essential for any movement that seeks to remake it. Movements must know their enemy. If they expend their energy on the wrong target, the opportunity for meaningful change is lost. History shows why privatization is the right target, how it forms the common foundation for the diverse dysfunctions and depredations of the modern internet. History shows us the face of the enemy.

Defeating this enemy is not a matter of putting history in reverse, if such a thing were even possible. Privatization was an act of reinvention: it made a small academic network into the modern internet. Deprivatization must be no less inventive. If privatization meant creating an internet that served the principle of profit maximization, deprivatization means creating an internet organized by the idea that people, not profit, should rule.

No single line of attack can achieve this end. Different strategies are needed for different layers. Down the stack, in the realm of the pipes, publicly and cooperatively owned community networks are the building blocks of a democratic internet. These networks can serve the communities exploited and excluded by the slumlords of the broadband cartel; instead of funneling money upward to executives and investors, they can focus on making service accessible and affordable. They can also give communities control over their operations, so that users and residents determine how infrastructure is run. Hundreds of such networks already exist across the United States, but they will have to be defended and extended with public support.

Up the stack, among the so-called platforms, the path to deprivatization is less linear. There is no equivalent of the community network. Here what's needed is the imaginative work of abolition. Two maneuvers are involved: first, shrinking the footprint of the online malls, which means making common cause with anti-monopoly advocates. Yet the goal of deprivatization is not an internet with more competitive markets, but an internet where markets matter less. This is why, while working to disassemble the online malls, we must also be assembling a constellation of alternatives that can lay claim to the space they currently occupy. And these must be real alternatives, not smaller or more entrepreneurial versions of the tech giants but institutions of a fundamentally different kind, engineered to curtail the power of the profit motive and to enshrine the practices and principles of democratic decision-making. Some are already emerging in rudimentary form—self-governing social media communities, worker-owned app-based services—but they will need to be refined and expanded through public investment. We will also need spaces that help new alternatives emerge, where people can collectively articulate their needs and construct the online worlds capable of meeting them.

The internet's inventors had hoped to invent a universal language. They succeeded, far beyond their furthest expectations. Their language was made for the US military, to help its assets adhere into a more effective war-making machine. But the primary purpose to which the language would ultimately be put was profit-making. It would serve the universality of ubiquitous commodification, of markets seeping into all available membranes. Yet other universalities are possible, and their outlines are occasionally visible in those moments of online life that elude or exceed market control. In such moments, people relate to one another as people—not as eyeballs or clicks or purchasing power or labor power.

Making it possible for the world's computers to talk to one another was an impressive technical achievement. Making this machinic conversation serve an end other than infinite accumulation will be a political one. It may seem unlikely, but so was the internet. History is filled with improbable turns that look inevitable in retrospect. The future will be too.

Acknowledgments

Thinking is social, and my first debt of gratitude is to the people who have let me think with them over the years. Foremost among these is my family at *Logic* magazine—Jim Fingal, Christa Hartsock, Moira Weigel, Xiaowei Wang, Alex Blasdel, and Celine Nguyen—and its contributors, many of whom I cite in these pages.

Nicole Aschoff and Shawn Gude edited pieces of mine for *Jacobin* that I drew on for this book. Merope Mills did the same at the *Guardian*. I'm grateful to them for their support and guidance. Quinn Slobodian gave feedback on portions of the manuscript and made it much better. My agent Molly Atlas helped shape this project and kept me from spiraling into space. My editor John Merrick proposed the idea for this book and edited it masterfully—I can't imagine a better collaborator. Will Tavlin fact-checked the manuscript with great meticulousness and remained remarkably cheerful throughout. Thanks also to my parents Peter and Mathea, my in-laws Bill and Kathy, Liz Daingerfield, Victor Pickard, Leo

Hollis, Tim Barker, Gabriel Winant, and Astra Taylor, all of whom contributed to the completion of this book.

To Zoe, Josephine, Moira: you got the dedication but I figured I'd give you the last word as well. To say you helped me write this book feels small; you are my conditions of possibility.

Notes

The notes are organized by paragraph. For each note I've listed the page number, followed by the first several words of the paragraph. The full note appears when the source is first cited; all subsequent citations of the source use short notes. Also, in order to save space, I've omitted URLs from almost all citations, since they should be findable online through a search of the title.

Preface: Among the Eels

ix, At the bottom of the ocean . . . This is a layer of the deep sea known as the abyssal zone, which extends from 9,800 to 19,700 feet. The fish with very large eyes is the abyssal grenadier. Many organisms in the abyssal zone glow through bioluminescence; the anglerfish is one of them. The octopus with no ink is the dumbo octopus, while the eel with the very large mouth is the pelican eel.

x, There are many such arteries . . . *MAREA:* "MAREA," Submarine Cable Networks, submarinenetworks.com; Winston Qiu,

"AWS Acquires a Fiber Pair on MAREA Cable System on IRU Basis," Submarine Cable Networks, January 21, 2019.

x, MAREA is a reminder . . . *"Civilization . . ."*: John Perry Barlow, "A Declaration of the Independence of Cyberspace," 1996.

x, One way is infrastructural. *"The contours . . ."*: Nicole Starosielski, *The Undersea Network* (Durham, NC: Duke University Press, 2015), 2. *Safer to follow known paths:* Karl Frederick Rauscher, *ROGUCCI Study Final Report* (New York: IEEE Communications Society, 2010), 93.

x, These earlier networks . . . Starosielski, *The Undersea Network*, 1–63.

xi, Connectivity is never neutral. *Galeano's veins:* Eduardo Galeano, *Open Veins of Latin America: Five Centuries of the Pillage of a Continent*, trans. Cedric Belfrage (New York: Monthly Review Press, 1973).

xiii, The internet has not . . . *Internet users:* Only 6.3 percent of the world's internet users now live in the United States. See Simon Kemp, "Digital 2021 April Statshot Report," DataReportal.

1. A People's History of the Internet

3, On November 22, 1977, a van . . . My discussion of the 1977 experiment draws from Don Nielson, "The SRI Van and Computer Internetworking," *Core Magazine* 3, no. 1 (February 2002): 2–6; Vinton Cerf, interview by Judy O'Neill, April 24, 1990, Charles Babbage Institute; Vinton Cerf, "How the Internet Came to Be," netvalley.com; Cade Metz, "Bob Kahn, The Bread Truck, and the Internet's First Communion," *Wired*, August 13, 2012; Cade Metz, "How a Bread Truck Invented the Internet," *The Register*, November 12, 2007; Vint Cerf and Bob Kahn, "30th Anniversary of Internetting with TCP/IP," filmed November 7, 2007, at the

Computer History Museum in Mountain View, California, YouTube; Barbara Denny, Paal Spilling, and Virginia Strazisar Travers, "Birth of the Internet," filmed November 7, 2007, at the Computer History Museum in Mountain View, California, YouTube; Vint Cerf et al., "Internet Milestone—30th Anniversary 3-Network Transmission," filmed November 7, 2007, at the Computer History Museum in Mountain View, California, https:// youtu.be/lapwgqzWC5g. Thanks also to Marc Weber and Eric Dennis of the Computer History Museum for providing photographs and video of the van from the museum's collection. *Recently became known as Silicon Valley:* in 1971, the journalist Don Hoefler popularized the term "Silicon Valley" in a series of articles for *Electronic News*, an industry trade publication.

4, **The first computer sat . . .** The computer in the van was an LSI-11; the custom packet radio equipment was built by Collins Radio. The location of the repeaters in the Bay Area packet radio network is shown in a map provided by the Computer History Museum. The Menlo Park building was the headquarters of the Stanford Research Institute (SRI). For a diagram that shows the path of the packets in the 1977 experiment, see Janet Abbate, *Inventing the Internet* (Cambridge, MA: MIT Press, 2000 [1999]), 132.

4, **In Menlo Park, the packets underwent . . .** At the SRI headquarters in Menlo Park, the packets hopped from the Bay Area packet radio network (PRNET) to the ARPANET, and then traveled to the Norwegian Seismic Array (NORSAR) facility in Kjeller, Norway. NORSAR was the first non-US node on ARPANET, and its cross-Atlantic link was via satellite: it used an earth station in Tanum, Sweden, to communicate through satellite to the Seismic Data Analysis Center (SDAC) in Alexandria, Virginia. This is where it gets a bit confusing: the packets traveled via satellite across the Atlantic while still on ARPANET when going to Europe, and then via satellite again on the way back—but this time using the Atlantic Packet Satellite Network (SATNET), not ARPANET. See ibid.; Cerf and Kahn, "30th Anniversary of Internetting with TCP/IP," YouTube, starts around 23:45; and "ARPANET Logical Map, March 1977," Computer History Museum.

4, The packets touched down . . . The facility outside Oslo was NORSAR. The satellite was part of the Intelsat IVA series of geostationary communications satellites owned by Intelsat, and it belonged to SATNET. The stop in London was the ARPANET node at University College London. See Abbate, *Inventing the Internet*, 132.

4, Etam wasn't far from . . . Etam Earth Station is about forty miles from Philippi, the site of the Battle of Philippi on June 3, 1861. *"An enchanted land":* "On a Mountain" (1909), in Ambrose Bierce, *A Sole Survivor: Bits of Autobiography,* ed. S. T. Joshi and David E. Schultz (Knoxville: University of Tennessee Press, 1998), 7.

5, Here, the packets returned . . . The Cambridge, Massachusetts, stop was the office of Bolt Beranek and Newman (BBN), while the final destination of the packets was the Information Sciences Institute (ISI) of the University of Southern California. See Abbate, *Inventing the Internet*, 132.

5, What was in the packets? Cerf, in "How the Internet Came to Be," claims the total distance traveled was 94,000 miles; Metz, in "How a Bread Truck Invented the Internet," puts it at 88,000 miles. The ping time of two seconds comes from Metz, as does the point about the lack of clarity regarding what message the packets contained.

6, That day in 1977 offered . . . My discussion of the origins of the internet relies heavily on Abbate, *Inventing the Internet* throughout.

Don Nielson, interview by author, June 4, 2016, also provided useful context.

6, Most of the innovation . . . *Government's role in Silicon Valley:* Mariana Mazzucato, *The Entrepreneurial State: Debunking Public vs. Private Sector Myths* (London: Anthem Press, 2013). *Importance of insulation from market forces for internet's development:* Abbate, *Inventing the Internet*, 145.

7, The internet was such an unlikely idea . . . *"Had first imagined . . .":* Nathan S. Newman, *Net Loss: Government, Technology and the Political Economy of Community in the Age of the Internet* (Berkeley: University of California Press, 2010 [2002]), 42.

7, One consequence was the creation . . . ARPA changed its name to DARPA in 1973, reverted to ARPA in 1993, and then changed back to DARPA in 1996. For simplicity's sake, I refer to the agency as DARPA throughout. My account of the origins of DARPA and ARPANET in this section draws from Abbate, *Inventing the Internet*, 7–81, and Johnny Ryan, *A History of the Internet and the Digital Future* (London: Reaktion Books, 2010), 23–30.

8, This network was ARPANET . . . *Air Force's attempt to persuade AT&T:* Ryan, *A History of the Internet*, 16–17. *DARPA's attempt to persuade AT&T:* Abbate, *Inventing the Internet*, 135, 195.

8, Luckily, as it turned out. At one point, BBN, the DARPA contractor who built ARPANET's packet-switching nodes (known as Interface Message Processors, or IMPs) refused to share the source code for its programs. This caused a conflict within the ARPANET contractor community, as related in Abbate, *Inventing the Internet*, 70–71, and Katie Hafner and Matthew Lyon, *Where the Wizards Stay Up Late: The Origins of the Internet* (New York: Simon and Schuster, 2006 [1996]), 233–34. DARPA ultimately forced BBN to share the source code.

9, The internet was created to win wars . . . My discussion of the

DARPA internetworking project in this section draws from Cerf, interview by O'Neill; Nielson, interview by author; Ryan Singel, "Vint Cerf: We Knew What We Were Unleashing on the World," *Wired*, April 23, 2012; Cerf and Kahn, "30th Anniversary of Internetting with TCP/IP," https://youtu.be/pSAtq43e0tQ; Abbate, *Inventing the Internet*, 113–45; Ryan, *A History of the Internet*, 31–44; Hafner and Lyon, *Where the Wizards Stay Up Late*, 219–37; and Barry M. Leiner et al., "A Brief History of the Internet," Internet Society, February 20, 1997, available at arxiv.org.

10, This required doing two things. The Bay Area packet radio network (PRNET) began operating in 1975, the same year that the Atlantic Packet Satellite Network (SATNET) project began, according to Abbate, *Inventing the Internet*, 118–21. For the military motivations for linking the wireless networks with ARPANET, see also Cerf and Kahn, "30th Anniversary of Internetting with TCP/IP," YouTube, starts around 13:54.

10, In response, the architects of the internet . . . The blueprint was Vint Cerf and Robert Kahn, "A Protocol for Packet Network Intercommunication," *IEEE Transactions on Communications* 22, no. 5 (May 1974): 637–48. *"A simple but . . .":* Ibid., 647. More context came from Vinton Cerf, email to author, June 30, 2016. At the time, Cerf was a professor at UCLA while Kahn was working at DARPA.

11, These rules would make it possible . . . *The 1976 experiment:* Ben Tarnoff, "How the Internet Was Invented," *Guardian*, July 15, 2016. The successful three-network experiment in 1977 is widely seen as more significant, since it confirmed that the internet protocol could be generalized across any network. According to Cerf, "if you could do it for three, you could do it for any number"; see Cerf and Kahn, "30th Anniversary of Internetting with TCP/IP," YouTube, starts around 6:12.

11, The design of these experiments . . . *"What we were simu-lating . . .":* Cerf, interview by O'Neill, 28.

11, The protocol developed by Cerf . . . The initial protocol developed by Cerf and Kahn was called the "Transmission Control Program" (TCP); see Cerf and Kahn, "A Protocol for Packet Network Intercommunication," and Vinton Cerf, Yogen Dalal, and Carl Sunshine, "Specification of Internet Transmission Control Program," RFC 675, December 1974. In 1978, the protocol was split into two parts: TCP (now the Transmission Control *Protocol*), which would handle communication between computers, and IP (the Internet Protocol), which would handle communication between networks. The two protocols became known as TCP/IP; see Abbate, *Inventing the Internet*, 130. Later, the TCP/IP protocol suite would grow to encompass other protocols, such as the File Transfer Protocol (FTP), which handles the transfer of files between computers, and the Hypertext Transfer Protocol (HTTP), which powers the World Wide Web.

12, This universality was created . . . *Around eight hundred bases in some eighty-five countries:* David Vine, *The United States of War: A Global History of America's Endless Conflicts, from Columbus to the Islamic State* (Berkeley: University of California Press, 2020), 2. *Ships, planes, tanks:* K. K. Rebecca Lai et al., "Is America's Military Big Enough?," *New York Times*, March 22, 2017. *Needed to be able to knit together:* Abbate, *Inventing the Internet*, 144.

12, The internet may have been created . . . The packet radio project remained largely experimental, per Abbate, *Inventing the Internet*, 120. The push to embrace TCP/IP was led by the Defense Communications Agency, which initially needed a way to interconnect ARPANET and another Pentagon network named AUTODIN II; see ibid., 133–42. This is also discussed in Nielson, interview by author.

12, TCP/IP was the answer. *"Was really the only . . .":* Quoted in Abbate, *Inventing the Internet*, 139. Switchover of ARPANET to TCP/IP: Ibid., 140–44; Hafner and Lyon, *Where the Wizards Stay Up Late*, 248–49; Ryan, *A History of the Internet*, 88–91. In 1983, the same year that ARPANET converted to TCP/IP, the military nodes split off from ARPANET to form a classified "MILNET"; the two networks were able to communicate through TCP/IP. *Formation of* the *internet:* Hafner and Lyon, *Where the Wizards Stay Up Late*, 244–45. The internet grew from fifteen networks in 1982 to more than four hundred in 1986, and this growth was driven by civilian local area networks (LANs) connecting to the internet, largely from university campuses; see Abbate, *Inventing the Internet*, 186–88.

13, The internet's usefulness soon . . . *Scientists demanding access:* Abbate, *Inventing the Internet*, 183. Ibid., 183–86 also discusses the Computer Science Research Network (CSNET), an NSF-funded network that aimed to bring the internet to computer scientists— academic, commercial, nonprofit, or government—across the country in the early 1980s; see also Hafner and Lyon, *Where the Wizards Stay Up Late*, 240–46. After CSNET, NSF developed NSFNET, which brought many more users online and took over from ARPANET as the internet's backbone in the late 1980s; see Abbate, *Inventing the Internet*, 191–95. ARPANET was decommissioned in 1990.

13, In this model, the river is useless . . . *Subsidizing regional networks:* Ibid. *Cost estimates:* Rajiv C. Shah and Jay P. Kesan, "The Privatization of the Internet's Backbone Network," *Journal of Broadcasting & Electronic Media* 51, no. 1 (2007): 93–94. Shah and Kesan derive their numbers from Jeffrey K. MacKie-Mason and Hal Varian, "The Economics of the Internet," *Dr. Dobb's Journal*, January 1994. MacKie-Mason and Varian put the total annual cost of NSFNET backbone operations and regional network subsidies at about $20 million, and add that this number was "less than 10 percent of the total U.S. expenditure on the Internet," which came from other public sources. Shah and Kesan arrived at their figures ($160 million and $1.6 billion) by multiplying the MacKie-Mason and Varian annual estimates by eight, because Merit ran the NSFNET backbone for eight years (from 1987 to 1995). The Shah and Kesan numbers are rough but remain the best available estimate.

14, In the 1970s, the government invented . . . Another important milestone in the growing availability of the internet was the implementation of TCP/IP on various operating systems. This effort was supported by the director of the Defense Communications Agency, who set up a "$20 million fund to finance computer manufacturers to implement TCP/IP on their machines," according to Abbate, *Inventing the Internet*, 143. DARPA also funded the implementation of TCP/IP in Berkeley's version of Unix, the widely adopted BSD (Berkeley Software Distribution), which appeared in a version released in 1983; see Hafner and Lyon, *Where the Wizards Stay Up Late*, 250.

14, Privatization didn't come out of nowhere. *Privatization was the plan all along:* Jay P. Kesan and Rajiv C. Shah, "Fool Us Once Shame on You—Fool Us Twice Shame on Us: What We Can Learn from the Privatizations of the Internet Backbone Network and the Domain Name System," *Washington University Law Quarterly* 79, no. 1 (2001): 117–19. *Original government reports:* Ibid., 130, 133. Kesan and Shah discuss two reports by the Office of Science and Technology Policy—"A Research and Development Strategy for High Performance Computing" (1987) and "The Federal High Performance Computing Program" (1989)—as well as the Federal Research Internet Coordinating Committee's "Program Plan" (1989).

14, By the early 1990s . . . Janet Abbate, "Privatizing the Internet: Competing Visions and Chaotic Events, 1987–1995," *IEEE Annals of the History of Computing* 32, no. 1 (January 2010): 14.

14, Clearly, people liked the internet. *NSFNET's AUP:* Ibid., 14–15; Abbate, *Inventing the Internet*, 196. For an analysis of the private sector making money off the internet, see Newman, *Net Loss*, 62–69. One example of industry monetization during the NSF-era internet is MCI Mail, which internet pioneer Vint Cerf helped develop. Cerf persuaded the NSF to allow MCI Mail to connect with the internet in 1988; CompuServe and Sprint would obtain permission as well. See Kesan and Shah, "Fool Us Once Shame on You," 112.

15, Still, the AUP did have . . . *Parallel system of private networks:* Hafner and Lyon, *Where the Wizards Stay Up Late*, 244; Abbate, *Inventing the Internet*, 197–99. In 1991, three commercial service providers—PSINet, CERFNet, and AlterNet—formed a nonprofit organization called the Commercial Internet Exchange (CIX), which set up a gateway to link the three networks; the CIX became, in Abbate's telling, "a commercial version of the Internet." *Role of government in spawning commercial providers:* Newman, *Net Loss*, 64–67.

15, This enthusiasm was driven . . . *Applications of early internet:* Abbate, *Inventing the Internet*, 212–13. These included Gopher and Usenet in addition to email.

16, The first website . . . *Rise of the World Wide Web and the creation of Mosaic:* Ibid., 213–18. My account of the NSF privatization process in this section draws from ibid., 195–205; Abbate, "Privatizing the Internet," 10–19; Kesan and Shah, "Fool Us Once Shame on You," 111–43; Shah and Kesan, "The Privatization of the Internet's Backbone Network," 93–106.

16, The move enraged the rest . . . *"Giving a federal . . .":* Quoted in Kesan and Shah, "Fool Us Once Shame on You," 125.

17, The goal was to promote . . . The five corporations that became the backbone providers in 1995 were UUNET, ANS, SprintLink, BBN, and MCI, with a combined market share of 90 percent; see Shah and Kesan, "The Privatization of the Internet's Backbone Network," 103. *Death of nonprofit regional networks: Newman, Net Loss,* 74.

18, What's striking about the privatization . . . *Depth of consensus on privatization:* Kesan and Shah, "Fool Us Once Shame on You," 117. *"I had people . . .":* Quoted in Yasha Levine, *Surveillance Valley: The Secret Military History of the Internet* (New York: PublicAffairs, 2018), 126.

18, Yet privatization also had . . . *Leased lines:* Abbate, "Privatizing the Internet," 17.

19, Perhaps nothing illustrates . . . *Gore's interest in digital technologies and legislative role in the internet:* Richard Wiggins, "Al Gore and the Creation of the Internet," *First Monday* 5, no. 10 (October 2000). *"The first elected . . .":* Robert Kahn and Vinton Cerf, "Al Gore and the Internet," October 1, 2000, initially circulated on the Politech mailing list. The money for NSFNET in the Gore Bill was allocated under the auspices of creating a "National Research and Education Network" (NREN), with NSFNET now reframed as an "interim NREN"; see Abbate, "Privatizing the Internet," 16.

20, Though a centrist, Gore believed . . . *Gore's motivations and public-private partnership:* Ibid.; Wiggins, "Al Gore and the Creation of the Internet." Gore began using the terms "data highway" and "information superhighway" in the mid-to-late 1980s. For more on the early internet politics of the first Clinton administration, see Daniel Greene, *The Promise of Access: Technology, Inequality, and the Political Economy of Hope* (Cambridge, MA: MIT Press, 2021), 38–42.

20, Yet after Gore entered . . . *Gore's shifting language:* Abbate,

"Privatizing the Internet," 17; Victor Pickard and David Elliot Berman, *After Net Neutrality: A New Deal for the Digital Age* (New Haven, CT: Yale University Press, 2019), 45–46; Kesan and Shah, "Fool Us Once Shame on You," 119. *Telecom contributions to DNC:* "So You Want to Buy a President," *PBS Frontline*, January 30, 1996, transcript available at pbs.org. Gore gave his speech on December 21, 1993, at the National Press Club in Washington, DC; the text is available at clintonwhitehouse6 .archives.gov.

20, If a centrist politician in a position . . . Inouye's bill was the National Public Telecommunications Infrastructure Act of 1994 (S. 2195), introduced in June 1994; the quotes come from the text of the bill, available at Congress.gov. The bill did qualify the obligations on telecoms somewhat: they would be reduced or eliminated if the provider's network had "sufficient open architecture, capacity, and nondiscriminatory access terms." That same year, Inouye also co-sponsored the Communications Act of 1994 (S. 1822), which initially included a clause from Inouye that mandated a similar set-aside of 20 percent. It was later reduced to 5 percent and service was to be provided not for free but at "incremental cost-based rates"; see Patricia Aufderheide, *Communications Policy and the Public Interest: The Telecommunications Act of 1996* (New York: The Guilford Press, 1999), 51–53, for an analysis and Congress.gov for the text of the bill. For more on Inouye, see Levine, *Surveillance Valley*, 126–27; Ernest F. Hollings, "Digital Technology, Rotary Laws," *New York Times*, June 13, 1994; Steve Farnsworth and James Love, "High Tech Needs 'MacNeil/Lehrer,' Too," *New York Times*, July 31, 1994. It's worth noting that Inouye was not the only one proposing a differential fee structure: the Antitrust and Communications Reform Act of 1994 (H.R. 3626) also directed telecoms to give "public service institutions" preferential rates. *Telecommunications Policy Roundtable*: Aufderheide, *Communications Policy and the Public Interest*, 45–6. *"Public lane on the information superhighway"*: Ibid., 51; People for the American Way and the Media Access Project, "Public Interest Groups Hail Introduction of Bill to Provide 'Public Lane' on the Information Superhighway,' " press release, June 15, 1994.

21, One source of inspiration . . . *Very cheap or even free postage*: US Postal Service, "Postage Rates for Periodicals: A Narrative History," June 2010. The comparison to the US Postal Service was made at the time by the Electronic Frontier Foundation, a member of the Telecommunications Policy Roundtable, at an NSF-sponsored conference devoted to discussing the NREN; see "Proceedings of the NREN Workshop (Monterey, California, September 16–18, 1992)," A147-A149, available at files.eric.ed.gov/fulltext/ED356768 .pdf. *CSNET charging industry laboratories more:* Kesan and Shah, "Fool Us Once Shame on You," 102–3. The Telecommunications Act of 1996 introduced the "E-Rate" program, which enables public libraries and schools to receive phone and internet service at discounted rates, subsidized by the Universal Service Fund, which is funded by surcharges on phone bills. But telecoms are notoriously bad at complying with the program's requirements, and routinely overcharge schools and libraries; see Jeff Gerth, "AT&T, Feds Neglect Low-Price Mandate Designed to Help Schools," ProPublica, May 1, 2012; Laura Meckler and Douglas MacMillan, "'There Has to Be an Accounting': Former AT&T Lawyer Says Company Systemically Overcharged Neediest Schools," *Washington Post*, March 18, 2021.

22, The idea didn't get far. *Chester quotes:* John Markoff, "The Media Business; New Coalition to Seek a Public Data Highway," *New York Times*, October 26, 1993.

22, Without a social movement . . . The "Framework for Global Electronic Commerce" is available at clintonwhitehouse4.archives.gov.

23, There was nothing in the technical . . . *Free-nets and Grundner's Corporation for Public Cybercasting:* Ashley Dunn, "Information Freeway?; Open Data Path Is Urged," *New York Times*, August 4, 1994; Ernie Smith, "The Tale of the Free-Net, the Cheap Way Dial-Up Users Got Online," *Vice*, January 20, 2018.

2. *The Plunder Continues*

24, But not everything . . . *Five major backbone providers in 1995:* Kesan and Shah, "Fool Us Once Shame on You," 150. Backbone providers are those that run Tier 1 networks, which are networks that can reach the entire internet via peering—that is, without purchasing transit. Since peering agreements are private, it's not public knowledge which networks are Tier 1. At minimum, the list of US-based Tier 1 networks include those run by AT&T, Verizon, Lumen Technologies, GTT Communications, Sprint, and Zayo Group. (Comcast essentially operates a Tier 1 network because it reaches the whole US through peering, though it must purchase transit overseas.) The five backbone providers in 1995 were UUNET, ANS, SprintLink, BBN, and MCI. In 1996 UUNET was acquired by WorldCom, which was bought by Verizon in 2006; SprintLink continues to operate as a Tier 1 network owned by Sprint; BBN's internet assets would be acquired by Level 3 Communications (now Lumen) in 2003; and MCI was acquired by WorldCom in 1998, eight years before Verizon's acquisition of WorldCom.

25, The terms of privatization . . . *Secrecy and lack of regulation of backbone interconnections:* Shah and Kesan, "The Privatization of the Internet's Backbone," 102–3; Kesan and Shah, "Fool Us Once

Shame on You," 147–51; Abbate, "Privatizing the Internet," 18; April Glaser and Seth Schoen, "Peering into the Soft Underbelly of Net Neutrality," Electronic Frontier Foundation, February 19, 2014; Martin Hannigan, "Interconnection Agreements at Scale: Secret or Simple?," APNIC, October 26, 2017.

25, The situation with internet service providers (ISPs) . . . *76 percent of all internet subscriptions and avoiding competition:* Pickard and Berman, *After Net Neutrality*, 58–59; Allan Holmes and Chris Zubak-Skees, "U.S. Internet Users Pay More and Have Fewer Choices Than Europeans," Center for Public Integrity, April 2, 2015.

25, These behemoths have benefited . . . My account of the origins of the common carrier concept and its application to telecommunications in this section draws from Eli M. Noam, "Beyond Liberalization II: The Impending Doom of Common Carriage," Columbia University Working Papers Server Project, March 15, 1994; Philip M. Nichols, "Redefining 'Common Carrier': The FCC's Attempt at Deregulation by Redefinition," *Duke Law Journal* 1987, no. 3 (June 1987): 501–20.

26, Sixty-two years later . . . My discussion of the Telecommunications Act of 1996 and the subsequent shifts in broadband regulation in this section draws from Pickard and Berman, *After Net Neutrality*, 25–68.

28, The victory may prove fleeting. Biden encouraged the FCC to adopt net neutrality rules similar to those implemented by the Obama-era FCC in his "Executive Order on Promoting Competition in the American Economy," July 9, 2021. *92 percent of Americans:* Pickard and Berman, *After Net Neutrality*, 48. The 2005 Supreme Court decision was *National Cable & Telecommunications Ass'n v. Brand X Internet Services;* see ibid., 29–30, 47–50.

28, Cutting big ISPs loose . . . Ibid., 39–44, 65–66.

29, These deals are well suited . . . *Six companies account for nearly half of internet traffic:* Sandvine, *Global Internet Phenomena Report 2019* (San Jose, CA: Sandvine, 2019), 17. *Netflix-Comcast interconnection deal:* Edward Wyatt and Noam Cohen, "Comcast and Netflix Reach Deal on Service," *New York Times*, February 23, 2014; Jon Brodkin, "Netflix Is Paying Comcast for Direct Connection to Network," *Ars Technica*, February 23, 2014. In addition to doing interconnections with ISPs at internet exchange points, Netflix also places its "Open Connect Appliances" (OCAs)—essentially, servers full of Netflix content—directly within ISP networks; see Nihit Tandon, "Netflix Content Distribution through Open Connect," APNIC, June 20, 2018. A note on my use of "Google": since a corporate restructuring in 2015, Google's parent company is called Alphabet, and Google is technically a subsidiary. But for simplicity's sake I use "Google" to refer to both the parent company and its subsidiaries throughout the book. I do the same with Facebook, which in late 2021 rebranded as Meta.

29, Finding a more direct . . . The interconnection of small and medium-sized networks is known as "donut peering"; the "hole" in the donut consists of the larger networks that are being bypassed. *Google Fiber:* David Anders, "Whatever Happened to Google Fiber?," CNET, March 5, 2021.

29, Content providers like Google . . . *Own or lease more than half of undersea bandwidth:* Adam Satariano, "How the Internet Travels Across Oceans," *New York Times*, March 10, 2019. *Google building its own undersea cables:* Jameson Zimmer, "Google Owns 63,605 Miles and 8.5% of Submarine Cables Worldwide," BroadbandNow, September 12, 2018.

30, The proponents of a . . . *"Innovation, expanded . . .":* The "Framework for Global Electronic Commerce" is available at clinton whitehouse4.archives.gov.

30, How well does . . . *Internet costs higher in US than in Europe or Asia:* Becky Chao and Claire Park, "The Cost of Connectivity 2020," New America, July 2020. *Twelfth in average connection speeds:* Ookla, "Speedtest Global Index," fixed broadband global average speeds, June 2021, available at speedtest.net. The American Customer Satisfaction Index records customer satisfaction scores by industry since 1995. In 2020, internet service providers received a score of 65 (out of 100), while airlines received a score of 75 and health insurers received a score of 72. The industry-specific scores are available at theacsi.org/acsi-benchmarks/benchmarks-by-industry.

31, The reason for the pitiful state . . . Comcast's CEO is Brian L. Roberts, and his total compensation for 2019 is provided in a DEF 14A (an SEC form) filed by Comcast on April 24, 2020, available at cmcsa.com/node/34631/html#toc781322_11. *Buybacks and dividends:* in 2017, Charter spent $13.2 billion on buybacks and Comcast announced $5 billion in buybacks, as well as another $5 billion for an increased annual dividend; see Pickard and Berman, *After Net Neutrality*, 68. In October 2018, Comcast announced it would pause buybacks owing to high debt levels stemming from its acquisition of the British media and telecom conglomerate Sky; buybacks were resumed in May 2021.

31, The result is large disparities . . . *Microsoft research:* Steve Lohr, "Digital Divide Is Wider Than We Think, Study Says," *New York Times*, December 4, 2018. *Disconnected are disproportionately rural and low-income:* Monica Anderson, "Mobile Technology and Home Broadband 2019," Pew Research Center, June 13, 2019. *A third of rural Americans:* Andrew Perrin, "Digital Gap between Rural and Nonrural America Persists," Pew Research Center, May 31, 2019. *Almost half of households with incomes below $30,000:* Monica Anderson and Madhumitha Kumar, "Digital Divide Persists Even as Lower-Income Americans Make Gains in Tech Adoption," Pew Research Center, May 7, 2019. *Especially Black and Latino households:* Andrew Perrin and Erica Turner, "Smartphones Help Blacks, Hispanics Bridge Some—but Not All—Digital Gaps with Whites," Pew Research Center, August 20, 2019. *"Digital redlining":* Communications Workers of America and the National Digital Inclusion Alliance, "AT&T's Digital Redlining: Leaving Communities Behind for Profit," October 2020.

31, Home broadband is not . . . *17 percent of US adults:* Anderson, "Mobile Technology and Home Broadband 2019." *2015 Pew survey:* Aaron Smith, "Searching for Work in the Digital Era," Pew Research Center, November 19, 2015.

32, The COVID-19 crisis greatly magnified . . . *Finding internet in the parking lot:* Tony Romm, "'It Shouldn't Take a Pandemic': Coronavirus Exposes Internet Inequality among US Students as Schools Close Their Doors," *Washington Post*, March 16, 2020; Cecilia Kang, "Parking Lots Have Become a Digital Lifeline," *New York Times*, May 5, 2020.

32, But not everyone could make it . . . *One in five school-age children:* Monica Anderson and Andrew Perrin, "Nearly One-in-Five Teens Can't Always Finish Their Homework Because of the Digital Divide," Pew Research, October 26, 2018.

33, "I hope that there is a lesson . . ." Quoted in Kang, "Parking Lots Have Become a Digital Lifeline."

33, Democracy is a form of life . . . *"Is the name . . .":* Wendy Brown, *Undoing the Demos: Neoliberalism's Stealth Revolution* (New York: Zone Books, 2015), 178.

33, The philosopher John Dewey once . . . *Dewey's understanding of freedom and "resources necessary . . .":* John Dewey and James Hayden Tufts, *Ethics* (New York: Henry Holt and Company, 1908), 437–38. For an analysis of Dewey's idea of positive freedom, see Robert B. Westbrook, *John Dewey and American Democracy* (Ithaca, NY: Cornell University Press, 1991), 43–51.

34, This power must be rooted . . . *"Across all the centres . . .":* Stuart Hall, "The State: Socialism's Old Caretaker" (1984), in *Selected Political Writings: The Great Moving Right Show and Other Essays,* ed. Sally Davison et al. (Durham, NC: Duke University Press, 2017), 237.

36, This makes capitalists . . . *"An inhuman power . . .":* Karl Marx, *Economic and Philosophical Manuscripts of 1844,* trans. Gregor Benton, available at marxists.org.

3. *The People's Pipes*

38, So Chattanoogans decided to take . . . "Chattanooga Vota Is for TVA Power," *New York Times,* March 13, 1935.

39, Seventy-five years later . . . *1 gigabit per second service:* EPB, "Our History," https://epb.com/about/history/. According to *Q1 2010 Akamai's State of the Internet Connectivity Report* (Cambridge, MA: Akamai Technologies, 2010), 10, average measured connection speeds in the US were 4.7 megabits per second at the time.

39, The story of the Gig began . . . My discussion of the Gig in this section draws from Evan Malmgren, "The New Sewer Socialists," *Logic,* December 1, 2017.

39, In the years since . . . *One of the most popular ISPs: Consumer Reports* has ranked EPB as the top American ISP twice in three years, per Karl Bode, "A Community-Run ISP Is the Highest Rated Broadband Company in America," *Vice,* August 14, 2018. *Discounted plan:* EPB, "EPB to Offer Discounted Internet for Low-Income Families," available at epb.com. *State law prohibiting utilities from selling services below cost:* Chris Brooks, "From Sewer Socialism to Server Socialism: Appalachia's Internet Revolution," *In These Times,* February 6, 2018.

40, While the Gig is especially well known . . . : *More than nine hundred communities:* Institute for Local Self-Reliance, "Community Network Map," available at muninetworks.org. The cooperatives were given low-cost loans as part of the Rural Electrification Act of 1936; the TVA had been created three years earlier, with the Tennessee Valley Authority Act of 1933.

40, Publicly and cooperatively owned . . . *Harvard researchers:* David Talbot, Kira Hessekiel, and Danielle Kehl, "Community-Owned Fiber Networks: Value Leaders in America," Berkman Klein Center for Internet and Society Research Publication, January 2018. *"Community-owned ISPs . . .":* Ibid., 11. The finding by the Harvard researchers is further substantiated by Chao and Park, "The Cost of Connectivity 2020."

41, This makes them uniquely effective . . . *Gigabit speeds in Nelson, Logan, and Kidder Counties:* BroadbandNow, "Internet Service in North Dakota," broadbandnow.com. According to ibid., 93.5 percent of North Dakotans have access to 1 gigabit broadband. Population numbers come from US Census Bureau estimates, July 1, 2019. *ILSR report:* Katie Kienbaum et al., "How Local Providers Built the Nation's Best Internet Access in Rural North Dakota," Institute for Local Self-Reliance, May 2020.

41, The backstory began . . . *North Dakota broadband:* Ibid. *"Our goal isn't . . .":* Robin Anderson, interview by Christopher Mitchell, Community Broadband Bits podcast, January 9, 2018, transcript available at muninetworks.org.

42, Crucially, this is not just . . . R. K. Upadhya, "Parliaments of the Earth," *Logic*, May 17, 2021; Michael Seto and Cheryl Chasin, "General Survey of I.R.C. 501(c)(12) Cooperatives and Examination of Current Issues," Internal Revenue Service, 2002.

43, A particularly powerful illustration . . . *City almost 80 percent*

Black: US Census Bureau estimates, July 1, 2019. *Detroit internet statistics:* Detroit Community Technology Project, "Equitable Internet Initiative," available at detroitcommunitytech.org.

43, Since 2016, organizers . . . My discussion of the Equitable Internet Initiative in this section draws from J. Gabriel Ware, "When They Couldn't Afford Internet Service, They Built Their Own," *YES!* magazine, March 26, 2018; Mozilla, "Connecting the Unconnected in Detroit," February 20, 2018; "Meet the People Building Their Own Internet in Detroit," *Vice: Motherboard*, November 16, 2017, YouTube; Rising Voices, "Building Resilience with Community Technology across the United States," February 3, 2019; Aaron Kalischer-Coggins, "How Detroit Residents Are Building Their Own Internet," *The Hill*, May 28, 2021; Rebecca Ruiz, "So Many People Don't Have Internet—and It's Not Their Fault," *Mashable*, April 6, 2021; DCTP staff member, interview by author, June 25, 2021.

44, But digital stewards aren't just technicians. *Curriculum that draws on Freire and Boggs:* Diana J. Nucera et al., eds., *Teaching Community Technology Handbook*, Detroit Community Technology Project, 2015. *"We are working towards . . .":* Detroit Community Technology Project, "Equitable Internet Initiative Working Principles," 2020.

44, Such an approach is a far cry . . . *"The access doctrine":* Greene, *The Promise of Access*.

45, The organizers in Detroit . . . *Serve as the basis for a movement:* "Equitable Internet Initiative Working Principles."

46, By serving excluded communities . . . *Restricted or banned in eighteen states:* Tyler Cooper, "Municipal Broadband Is Restricted in 18 States across the U.S. in 2021," BroadbandNow, May 3, 2021. *Comcast's attempt to derail the Gig:* "Comcast Sues EPB in Hamilton County on Eve of Bond Issue," *Chattanoogan.com*, April 22, 2008.

46, The intensity with which the broadband giants . . . *"What the broadband . . .":* Pickard and Berman, *After Net Neutrality,* 110.

48, Defending community networks begins . . . The Sixth Circuit Court of Appeals overturned the FCC's preemption order in *Tennessee v. FCC* in 2016; for an analysis, see John T. Cobb, "Broad-Banned: The FCC's Preemption of State Limits on Municipal Broadband and the Clear Statement Rule," *Emory Law Journal* 68, no. 2 (2018): 406–39. Congressional bills that would prohibit state and local governments from banning municipal broadband are periodically introduced, so far without success; for example, the Community Broadband Act of 2017 (S. 742) and the Community Broadband Act of 2019 (H.R. 2785).

48, Both Bernie Sanders and Elizabeth Warren . . . *Warren plan:* Elizabeth Warren, "My Plan to Invest in Rural America," August 7, 2019. *Sanders plan:* Bernie Sanders, "High-Speed Internet for All," December 2019.

49, Municipal governments also have . . . The DC network is called DC-Net, while the program that serves community non-profits is called DC Columbia Community Access Network (DC-CAN); see "About DC-Net," dcnet.dc.gov, and "DC-CAN FAQs," dcnet.dc.gov. *DC franchise agreements:* Aaron Wiener, "Fiber-Optical Illusion," *Washington City Paper,* May 2, 2013.

50, Along these lines . . . *"Embrace democratic . . .":* Thomas M. Hanna, Mathew Lawrence, Adrienne Buller, and Miriam Brett, "Democratic Digital Infrastructure," Common Wealth and The Democracy Collaborative, May 18, 2020, 33.

50, A further advantage of public funding . . . *Half of those who have no home broadband:* Anderson, "Mobile Technology and Home Broadband 2019."

50, What if they did . . . *"Move towards providing . . .":* Hanna et al., "Democratic Digital Infrastructure," 33.

51, Making this more . . . *Fiber Broadband Association study:* Masha Zager, "To Reduce Network Operating Expenses, Choose FTTH," *Broadband Communities,* July 2020.

51, Throwing money at community networks . . . *Nearly 20 million state and local government workers:* US Bureau of Labor Statistics, "Employment by Major Industry Sector," available at bls.gov.

52, Hospitals and universities also tend . . . *2021 study:* Grant Suneson, "The Largest Employer in Every State," *24/7 Wall St.,* April 8, 2021.

52, These relationships wouldn't have to be . . . *"Democratic collective . . .":* Joe Guinan and Martin O'Neill, *The Case for Community Wealth Building* (Cambridge: Polity, 2020), 2. See ibid., 9–16, for the Cleveland and Preston experiments and ibid., 25–26, for the role of anchor institutions.

53, Not all community networks can . . . *Red Hook's mesh network:* Noam Cohen, "Red Hook's Cutting-Edge Wireless Network," *New York Times,* August 22, 2014. Another interesting approach is the "condominium model" for fiber ownership, which involves neighborhood-run broadband; see Derek Slater and Tim Wu, "Homes with Tails: What If You Could Own Your Internet Connection?," *CommLaw Conspectus: Journal of Communications Law and Technology Policy* 18 (2009): 67–95.

54, Ideally, we could come up . . . Some potential regional and national interventions are the federal "Fiber for All" plan recommended in Pickard and Berman, *After Net Neutrality,* 112–13; the postal ISP idea explored in Paris Marx, "Build Socialism through the Post Office," *Jacobin,* April 15, 2020; and Abdul El-Sayed's proposal for a statewide public ISP, "MI-Fi," which he unveiled when running for Michigan's governor in 2018.

55, The center of the system . . . *"The interim internet":* Andrew Blum, interview by Christopher Mitchell, Community Broadband

Bits podcast, February 2, 2016, transcript available at muninetworks .org. See also Andrew Blum, *Tubes: A Journey to the Center of the Internet* (New York: HarperCollins, 2012). Chattanooga's EPB interconnects with Level 3, Hurricane Electric, and Cogent Communications; see bgp.he.net/AS26827#_asinfo.

55, In fact, this may become . . . Comcast, Charter, Verizon, and AT&T account for 76 percent of all internet subscriptions in the country; see Pickard and Berman, *After Net Neutrality*, 58–59. Verizon, AT&T, and Comcast are the companies that also operate backbones.

56, The Green New Deal might offer . . . *"When clouds soften . . .":* Kate Aronoff, Alyssa Battistoni, Daniel Aldana Cohen, and Thea Riofrancos, *A Planet to Win: Why We Need a Green New Deal* (London: Verso, 2019), 107. *Thousands of miles of unused "dark" fiber*: There are two main reasons that so much unused fiber exists. The first is the legacy of overbuilding during the dot-com boom. The second is the fact that overbuilding is the norm: fiber is typically laid with more capacity than will be immediately used due to the expense associated with installation.

56, This may seem impractical . . . The original German line from *Dantons Tod* (1835) reads, "Wer eine Revolution zur Hälfte vollendet, gräbt sich selbst sein Grab."

4. From Below

59, To begin with, it's worth pointing out . . . DCTP staff member, interview by author, June 25, 2021.

59, There are a number of federal programs . . . For a description of the major government broadband funding programs, see BroadbandNow, "National Broadband Map," available at broadbandnow.com.

59, The problem with this approach . . . *CenturyLink:* Jon Brodkin, "CenturyLink, Frontier Took FCC Cash, Failed to Deploy All Required Broadband," *Ars Technica*, January 23, 2020. The $505.7 million in annual support came from the Connect America Fund, which is a program within the Universal Service Fund. Century-Link's CEO is Jeffrey Storey. *His 2018 compensation:* Sarah Barry James and Waqar Jamshed, "CenturyLink CEO Compensation Tops List among Largest Pay TV Providers," S&P Global Market Intelligence, May 21, 2019. In September 2020, CenturyLink changed its name to Lumen Technologies.

60, The amount of money involved . . . *FCC and USDA numbers and "the mechanism of . . .":* Daniel A. Hanley, "Universal Broadband, Now More Than Ever," *American Prospect*, October 2, 2020.

60, This money would be better spent . . . Facebook revenue in 2019 was $70.70 billion, while Google's was $160.74 billion. *"They are responsible . . .":* David Elliot Berman, "We Need Broadband Internet for All," *Jacobin*, December 23, 2019.

61, Competition is routinely presented . . . *Multiple studies:* Gabor Molnar and Scott J. Savage. "Market Structure and Broadband Internet Quality," *Journal of Industrial Economics* 65, no. 1 (2017): 73–104, and Holmes and Zubak-Skees, "US Internet Users Pay More."

61, But competition is . . . Dan Mahoney and Greg Rafert, "Broadband Competition Helps to Drive Lower Prices and Faster Download Speeds for U.S. Residential Consumers," Analysis Group, November 2016, 24.

62, These practices reflect another problem . . . In a 2017 paper published by a team of American and Taiwanese scholars, they report their finding that "even under competitive pressure from a rival ISP, an ISP still has the incentive and the ability to enforce charging content providers for priority delivery of content." See Hong Guo, Subhajyoti Bandyopadhyay, Arthur Lim, Yu-Chen

Yang, and Hsing Kenneth Cheng, "Effects of Competition among Internet Service Providers and Content Providers on the Net Neutrality Debate," *MIS Quarterly* 41, no. 2 (2017): 353–70.

64, This is another example . . . *"Configures human beings . . .":* Brown, *Undoing the Demos*, 31. *"By nature . . .":* Aristotle, *Politics*, quoted in ibid., 87.

64, One final area of concern . . . India's internet shutdowns since 2012 are mapped in SFLC.IN's Internet Shutdown Tracker, available at internetshutdowns.in. India shuts down the internet more than any other country; see Marc Daniel Davies, "Internet Shutdowns Plunged Millions into 'Digital Darkness' Last Year," *Bloomberg*, March 3, 2021.

65, But state spying, censorship, and shutdowns . . . *NSA tapping fiber-optic cables:* Craig Timberg, "NSA Slide Shows Surveillance of Undersea Cables," *Washington Post*, July 10, 2013, and Olga Khazan, "The Creepy, Long-Standing Practice of Undersea Cable Tapping," *The Atlantic*, July 16, 2013.

65, The post office was the first . . . *Postal confidentiality:* Anuj C. Desai, "Wiretapping before the Wires: The Post Office and the Birth of Communications Privacy," *Stanford Law Review* 60, no. 2 (2007): 553–94. *"The ideological premise . . .":* Ibid., 565.

66, Laws and regulations are useful . . . *"Inclusive and . . .":* Andrew Cumbers and Thomas M. Hanna, "Constructing the Democratic Public Enterprise," Democracy Collaborative and the University of Glasgow, June 2019, 5. *"Is rooted in . . .":* Hall, "The State: Socialism's Old Caretaker," 236.

5. Up the Stack

71, On Labor Day weekend in 1995 . . . *Omidyar's background and origins of AuctionWeb:* Adam Cohen, *The Perfect Store: Inside eBay*

(Boston: Little, Brown, 2003 [2002]), 3–21. The startup Omidyar co-founded was initially called the Ink Development Corporation, later renamed eShop; Microsoft bought it in 1996. The name of the company he worked for that made software for handheld computers was General Magic.

71, Buying and selling was still . . . *Gates memo:* Bill Gates, "The Internet Tidal Wave," May 26, 1995. The memo surfaced during the Department of Justice antitrust investigation of Microsoft, and is available at justice.gov/sites/default/files/atr/legacy/2006/03/03/20.pdf.

72, If the internet of 1995 inspired . . . *Nearly 45 million users:* Internet Live Stats, available at internetlivestats.com. According to ibid., there were 25,454,590 internet users in 1994.

72, But how exactly? *Number of websites:* Ibid.

73, Omidyar was fond . . . *Omidyar's early internet days:* Cohen, *The Perfect Store,* 7, 19. *"Wallets and eyeballs":* Ibid., 7.

73, "I wanted to do something . . ." *"I wanted to . . .":* Quoted in ibid. *AuctionWeb as perfect market:* Ibid., 6–7. See also Pierre Omidyar, "How Pierre Omidyar Turned an Idealistic Notion into Billions of Dollars," *Inc.,* December 2013/January 2014.

73, The site grew quickly. *Items listed for sale:* Cohen, *The Perfect Store,* 23. *Web hosting fee increase and AuctionWeb turning a profit:* Ibid., 25–26. Later, in addition to taking a cut of transactions, eBay would introduce listing fees.

74, But the perfect market . . . *"Give praise . . .":* The letter from Omidyar, dated February 26, 1996, is viewable in a screenshot of AuctionWeb from 1997 at internetlivestats.com/img/auctionweb-(ebay)-1995.gif. *Feedback forum:* Cohen, *The Perfect Store,* 27–8, and Michele White, *Buy It Now: Lessons from eBay* (Durham, NC: Duke University Press, 2012), 43–46. Shortly after creating the feedback forum, Omidyar also launched a bulletin board where buyers and sellers could ask one another for advice, from the best strategy for placing bids to the best way to ship goods.

74, By the summer of 1996 . . . *$10,000 a month:* Cohen, *The Perfect Store,* 29.

75, None of the metaphors . . . Tarleton Gillespie, "The Politics of 'Platforms,'" *New Media and Society* 12, no. 3 (2010): 347–64.

76, This was the central focus . . . *Tens of thousands of startups:* "50,000 new ventures were formed to exploit the commercialization of the Internet from 1998–2002," according to Brent D. Goldfarb, David A. Kirsch, and Michael D. Pfarrer, "Searching for Ghosts: Business Survival, Unmeasured Entrepreneurial Activity and Private Equity Investment in the Dot-Com Era," Robert H. Smith School Research Paper No. RHS 06-027, October 12, 2005, 2. *Hundreds of billions of dollars:* Ibid. reports that "24,000 firms raised $256 billion from formal and informal investors from 1996–2002." Total US venture-capital investments were $8 billion in 1995 and $105.2 billion in 2000; see Yixi Ning, Wei Wang, and Bo Yu, "The Driving Forces of Venture Capital Investments," *Small Business Economics* 44, no. 2 (2005): 323. *Hundreds of dot-com companies went public:* According to Carlota Perez, "The Double Bubble at the Turn of the Century: Technological Roots and Structural Implications," CFAP/CERF Working Paper No. 31, May 10, 2009, 7, the peak of the dot-com IPO mania was reached in 1999, when almost six hundred information and telecommunications technology firms went public. *Worth more than $5 trillion:* Ibid., 9.

76, Yet profits mostly failed . . . *Grow fast and monetize later:* Nick Srnicek, *Platform Capitalism* (Cambridge: Polity, 2017), 21. *"The internet has yet . . .":* Quoted in Tim Hwang, *Subprime Attention Crisis: Advertising and the Time Bomb at the Heart of the Internet* (New York: FSG Originals x Logic, 2020), 9. See also Seth

Schiesel, "Payoff Still Elusive in Internet Gold Rush," *New York Times,* January 2, 1997. *Nasdaq's average price-earnings ratio:* Perez, "The Double Bubble at the Turn of the Century," 12.

77, The next year . . . *"It's rare to see . . .":* David Kleinbard, "The $1.7 Trillion Dot.com Lesson," *CNNMoney,* November 9, 2000.

77, Today, the era is typically . . . *"Irrational exuberance":* Greenspan used the phrase in a speech to the American Enterprise Institute on December 5, 1996. See "Excerpt from the Speech by Greenspan," *New York Times,* December 7, 1996, and Richard W. Stevenson, "A Buried Message Loudly Heard," *New York Times,* December 7, 1996. *Pets.com:* Jennifer Thornton and Sunny Marche, "Sorting through the Dot Bomb Rubble: How Did the High-Profile e-Tailers Fail?," *International Journal of Information Management* 23, no. 2 (April 2003): 128, 130.

77, But it would be a mistake . . . *Many of the same ideas would resurface:* For example, Webvan was a forerunner of Instacart and Amazon's grocery delivery service, and even Pets.com has been reincarnated as Chewy.

78, In his analysis of capitalist . . . *Marx on "formal" and "real" subsumption:* "The Results of the Direct Production Process," included in Karl Marx, *Capital: A Critique of Political Economy, Volume One,* trans. Ben Fowkes (London: Penguin Books, 1990 [1976]), 1019–38.

78, This is a useful lens . . . For a slightly different discussion of formal subsumption and real subsumption within the context of the internet, see Gavin Mueller, *Breaking Things at Work: The Luddites Are Right about Why You Hate Your Job* (London: Verso, 2021), 108–9.

79, In this, the internet followed . . . *Email:* Abbate, *Inventing the Internet,* 106–10; Hafner and Lyon, *Where the Wizards Stay Up Late,* 187–218. *Three-quarters of all network traffic:* Ibid., 194. *Early online communities:* Ryan, *A History of the Internet,* 74–87.

80, Email was more than just . . . *"I designed it . . .":* Tim Berners-Lee, *Weaving the Web* (New York: HarperBusiness, 2000 [1999]), 123.

80, Community is what Omidyar . . . *Nettime:* Evan Malmgren, "Specter in the Machine," *Logic,* December 20, 2020. *Omidyar's disdain for cheesy web commercialization:* Cohen, *The Perfect Store,* 7.

80, eBay, by contrast . . . *Importance of eBay as "community":* White, *Buy It Now,* 26–39.

81, This wasn't an entirely . . . Bill Gates, with Nathan Myhrvold and Peter Rinearson, *The Road Ahead* (New York: Viking, 1995), 6.

81, Combining the community with the market . . . *Encouraged to perform unpaid activities:* As White observes in *Buy It Now,* 31, "eBay's community discourse gets members to work for free." Advice on shipping was provided in the bulletin board, launched shortly after the feedback forum.

82, A second, related strength . . . *Pets.com paid a fortune:* "Products such as kitty litter and dog food are low margin products at the outset. When the company sent them across the country and charged only $2 per pound for anything over 11 pounds, this created money-losing transactions," per Thornton and Marche, "Sorting through the Dot Bomb Rubble," 127.

82, But both the benefits . . . *Kashkooli's study:* Keyvan Alan Kashkooli, "The Making of a Modern Market: eBay.com," PhD diss., University of California, Berkeley, 2010. See pages 1–17 for a summary of the argument.

83, This laissez-faire approach . . . *Manipulation of feedback forum:* Ibid., 28–31. *"Despite its initial . . .":* Ibid., 16.

83, These three elements . . . My analysis is informed by Nick Srnicek, who identifies four characteristics of "platforms": they are intermediaries, they "produce and are reliant on 'network effects,'" they often use "cross-subsidisation" to reduce the price of a good or service, and they have "a designed core architecture that governs the interaction possibilities"; see Srnicek, *Platform Capitalism*, 36–48.

6. Online Malls

85, Back in 1993 . . . *"A virtual . . .":* Quoted in John Markoff, "The Media Business; New Coalition to Seek a Public Data Highway," *New York Times*, October 26, 1993. *Shopping malls metaphor:* Jathan Sadowski, "The Internet of Landlords: Digital Platforms and New Mechanisms of Rentier Capitalism," *Antipode* 52, no. 2 (2020): 562–80. For an earlier analysis of online commodification that uses the shopping mall metaphor, see Jennifer S. Light, "Developing the Virtual Landscape," *Environment and Planning D: Society and Space* 14 (1996): 127–31.

85, The first modern shopping mall . . . *"Rich public . . .":* Quoted in M. Jeffrey Hardwick, *Mall Maker: Victor Gruen, Architect of an American Dream* (Philadelphia: University of Pennsylvania Press, 2004), 133. *"Outlet for that . . .":* Victor Gruen and Laurence P. Smith, "Shopping Centers: The New Building Type," *Progressive Architecture* (June 1952): 67–109.

86, Real malls are in the . . . On online mall rent-seeking, in addition to Sadowski, "The Internet of Landlords," see Paul Langley and Andrew Leyshon, "Platform Capitalism: The Intermediation and Capitalization of Digital Economic Circulation," *Finance and Society* 3, no. 1 (2017): 11–31.

88, In 1998, the same year . . . Steven Levy, *In the Plex: How Google Thinks, Works, and Shapes Our Lives* (New York: Simon and Schuster, 2011), 32–34. The paper was Sergey Brin and Lawrence Page, "The Anatomy of a Large-Scale Hypertextual Web Search Engine," *Computer Networks and ISDN Systems* 30 (1998): 107–17.

88, Having too much data . . . IPv4, introduced in 1981, uses a 32-bit address space, which allows for approximately 4.3 billion addresses. IPv4 is still used to route most internet traffic, despite the introduction of IPv6, which uses 128 bits and thus has a much larger number of addresses available. *Travers thinking 65,536 would be enough:* Travers's remarks in "Barbara Denny, Paal Spilling, and Virginia Strazisar Travers," YouTube, starts around 23:42. Travers says, "I distinctly remember sitting there saying, 'Well, it took us six months to get the last two [computers] connected, so we're going to need 216 here? I don't think in my lifetime.' "

88, In the 1990s . . . *Tens of millions joining the internet each year:* according to Internet Live Stats, there were 25,454,590 internet users in 1994, 44,838,900 in 1995, 77,433,860 in 1996, and 120,758,310 in 1997. *Millions of miles of fiber-optic cable:* Srnicek, *Platform Capitalism*, 22. *Number of websites growing nearly 1,000 percent:* Internet Live Stats shows 23,500 websites in 1995 and 257,601 in 1996.

89, In theory, more information . . . *Spammy results:* See the discussion of the AltaVista search engine in Levy, *In the Plex*, 24–25.

89, This was the challenge . . . In "The Anatomy of a Large-Scale Hypertextual Web Search Engine," Page and Brin write that their research was supported by the NSF, DARPA, NASA, Interval Research, and "the industrial partners of the Stanford Digital Libraries Project." *"The number of documents . . .":* Ibid., 108. The method outlined in the paper, called PageRank, drew on a technique known as citation analysis; see Safiya Umoja Noble, *Algorithms of Oppression: How Search Engines Reinforce Racism* (New York: New York University Press, 2018), 38–41.

89, But as Google moved off-campus . . . *More than 4 million searches a day:* Sergey Brin, interview by Leslie Walker, WashingtonPost.com, November 4, 1999.

90, The company began using . . . Levy identifies Google engineer Amit Patel as the first one who "realized the value of Google's logs"; see *In the Plex*, 45–49. This is seconded in Douglas Edwards, *I'm Feeling Lucky: The Confessions of Google Employee Number 59* (Boston: Houghton Mifflin Harcourt, 2011), which states that Patel's first major project at Google involved creating "a rudimentary system to make sense of the logs that recorded user interactions with our site," though according to Edwards, it would take three more years of development before Google's logs analytics tool, "Sawmill," was "activated" in 2003; see 344–45. See also Shoshana Zuboff, *The Age of Surveillance Capitalism: The Fight for a Human Future at the New Frontier of Power* (New York: PublicAffairs, 2019), 67–70.

90, Google had been selling . . . Google began selling ads in July 1999; see Levy, *In the Plex*, 78. *Sandberg and Schmidt:* Ibid., 99. *Page and Brin's hatred for ads:* Ibid., 83. When Page and Brin met with Jeff Bezos, an early Google investor, in 1998, they told him they would never put ads on the site; see ibid., 34. Google's initial business plan anticipated three revenue streams: licensing search technology to other sites, selling a hardware device that enabled other companies to perform internal searches, and advertising. But in the early days, Google expected to earn most of its revenue through licensing; see ibid., 77, 84. *"We really couldn't . . .":* Quoted in John Battelle, *The Search: How Google and Its Rivals Rewrote the Rules of Business and Transformed Our Culture* (Boston: Nicholas Brealey Publishing, 2005), 93.

90, This changed in 2002 . . . AdWords originally appeared in 2000, but an improved version called AdWords Select launched in 2002, and the original was soon discontinued. AdWords Select used a quality score, as well as an auction mechanism; see Levy, *In the Plex*, 85–93, and Hwang, *Subprime Attention Crisis*, 36–41.

AdWords Select was later renamed AdWords, and is now known as Google Ads. Interestingly, Levy claims that a quality score based on click-through rate (CTR) was already active in the original AdWords from 2000, though it's safe to say that ad quality became more important with the introduction of AdWords Select in 2002; see *In the Plex*, 86.

90, How was the quality score calculated? *Calculation of quality score:* Levy, *In the Plex*, 91–92; Zuboff, *The Age of Surveillance Capitalism*, 82–83; Bernard J. Jansen and Tracy Mullen, "Sponsored Search: An Overview of the Concept, History, and Technology," *International Journal of Electronic Business* 6, no. 2 (2008): 120–23; Frederick Vallaeys, "AdWords Quality Score: All You Need to Know from a Former Googler," KlientBoost, klientboost.com. Vallaeys says that when he joined Google in 2002, the display order of ads was determined by a simple formula: bid multiplied by click-through rate (CTR). Around 2005, the formula became bid multiplied by *predicted* CTR, and Google renamed this latter measure the "AdWords Quality Score," which was soon expanded to incorporate other factors.

91, The beauty of the arrangement . . . Levy, *In the Plex*, 92–93.

92, In *The Age of Surveillance Capitalism* . . . *"Behavioral surplus":* Zuboff, *The Age of Surveillance*, 63–97. *"Google had discovered . . .":* Ibid., 93.

92, This wasn't the first time . . . *Pioneering scholar of surveillance studies:* Oscar H. Gandy Jr., *The Panoptic Sort: A Political Economy of Personal Information* (Oxford: Oxford University Press, 2021 [1993]).

93, In short, in the early . . . The other important development at Google in this period was the launch of AdSense in 2003, which extended the AdWords model into the wider web by enabling site owners to sell space to advertisers and split the money with Google. See Levy, *In the Plex*, 103–8.

93, The innovations of 2002 . . . *"Black boxes inside . . .":* Shoshana Wodinsky, "It Doesn't Matter Who Owns TikTok," *Gizmodo,* August 7, 2020. For more on ad auctions, see Shengwu Li, interview by *Logic,* "The Art of Eyeball Harvesting: Shengwu Li on Online Advertising," *Logic,* January 1, 2019. Google plans to upend the existing web advertising ecosystem by eliminating support for third-party tracking cookies from its popular Chrome browser and introducing a new ad-targeting technique, which is expected to be implemented in 2023; see Shoshana Wodinsky, "Google's Quest to Kill the Cookie Is Creating a Privacy Shitshow," *Gizmodo,* June 11, 2021. Google has promoted this move as a privacy-friendly change, but it remains to be seen whether the new paradigm will involve significantly less surveillance.

93, Google remains the apex predator . . . *Google and Facebook's shares of the digital ad market:* Alexandra Bruell, "Amazon Surpasses 10% of U.S. Digital Ad Market Share," *Wall Street Journal,* April 6, 2021.

94, What characterized these sites . . . *"The key to . . .":* Tim O'Reilly, "What Is Web 2.0: Design Patterns and Business Models for the Next Generation of Software," September 30, 2005. For an analysis of Web 2.0 and the rise of the "platform," see Anne Helmond, "The Platformization of the Web: Making Web Data Platform Ready," *Social Media + Society* 1, no. 2 (July 2015): 1–11. For Web 2.0 and the rise of social media, see José van Dijck, *The Culture of Connectivity: A Critical History of Social Media* (Oxford: Oxford University Press, 2013).

94, These enclosures would be particularly . . . *"Typhoid Mary":* Zuboff, *The Age of Surveillance Capitalism,* 92.

94, The online mall of social media . . . *Maximize engagement:* Karen Hao, "How Facebook Got Addicted to Spreading Misinformation," *MIT Technology Review,* March 11, 2021. *Impose a* *"grammar"*: Philip E. Agre, "Surveillance and Capture: Two Models of Privacy," *The Information Society* 10, no. 2 (1994): 101–27.

95, A grammar is not a straitjacket . . . *"Just as the . . ."*: Ibid., 117.

96, Just because these ads . . . *"Advertising* packages . . .": Hwang, *Subprime Attention Crisis*, 76.

96, Immense amounts of data . . . Zuboff on mind control: See for example Zuboff, *The Age of Surveillance Capitalism*, 293–328, and Shoshana Zuboff, "You Are Now Remotely Controlled," *New York Times*, January 24, 2020.

97, This is not to downplay . . . *"Attention is commodified . . ."*: Ibid., 42–43.

7. Elastic Empires

98, This wasn't as easy . . . Founded in 1998, Kozmo.com was an e-commerce company that offered free one-hour delivery of various products to customers in nine urban markets; one of the products they offered was Starbucks coffee. Kozmo ceased operations in 2001. Founded in 1996, Webvan was an online grocery business that did home delivery and operated in ten urban markets; it went bankrupt in 2001. Finally, Pets.com was founded in 1998 and sold pet supplies to customers; it closed in 2000. Logistics challenges were a common theme in the failure of all three: see John C. Wu, "Anatomy of a Dot-Com," *Supply Chain Management Review* 5, no. 6 (November/December 2001): 42–50; William Aspray, George Royer, and Melissa G. Ocepek, *Food in the Internet Age* (New York: Springer Publishing, 2013), 25–35; Thornton and Marche, "Sorting through the Dot Bomb Rubble," 121–38.

99, Yet an early observer . . . *"This is horrible . . ."*: Quoted in Brad Stone, *The Everything Store: Jeff Bezos and the Age of Amazon* (New York: Back Bay Books, 2014 [2013]), 78.

99, Amazon's margins were made ... *Amazon's dot-com-crash blues:* Ibid., 100–35. *"Most observers . . .":* Ibid., 100.

100, Amazon crawled out ... *Lawsuit:* Patrick M. Reilly, "Barnes & Noble Sues Amazon over Rival's Book-Selling Claims," *Wall Street Journal,* May 13, 1997.

100, The first step came ... *Launch of Marketplace:* Stone, *The Everything Store,* 115–16. Amazon had previously experimented with hosting third-party sales through Amazon Auctions and zShops; neither was a success. *Sales figures for first four months:* Amazon.com, "Amazon Marketplace a Winner for Customers, Sellers and Industry; New Service Grows over 200 Percent in First Four Months," March 19, 2001. *Amazon becoming profitable:* Stone, *The Everything Store,* 134. Amazon's first profitable quarter was Q4 2001.

100, In the coming years ... *eBay vs Amazon:* Kashkooli, "The Making of a Modern Market," 75–82; Stone, *The Everything Store,* 263–65. *$14.8 billion in sales:* Ibid., 265. *More than doubled between 2000 and 2009:* Kashkooli, "The Making of a Modern Market," 75.

101, Building a third-party marketplace ... *Third-party sellers were responsible for most of the sales:* "Share of paid units sold by third-party sellers on Amazon platform as of 2nd quarter 2021," Statista, August 11, 2021. The tipping point came in Q2 2017, when the share of paid units sold by third-party sellers hit 51 percent. As of Q1 2021, the third-party share is 55 percent. For a breakdown of the costs associated with selling on Amazon, see sell.amazon.com/pricing.html. *Amazon begins giving out business loans:* See sell.amazon.com/programs/amazon-lending.html. *A miniature marketplace for attention:* Benedict Evans, "Does Amazon Make More from Ads Than AWS?," March 14, 2021. Amazon's share of the US digital ad market grew to 10.3 percent in 2020; see Alexandra Bruell, "Amazon Surpasses 10% of U.S. Digital Ad Market Share," *Wall Street Journal,* April 6, 2021.

101, But third-party sellers . . . *"They happen . . .":* Quoted in Leo Kelion, "Why Amazon Knows So Much about You," BBC News, 2020.

101, This identity had started . . . *More technical emphasis:* Stone, *The Everything Store,* 193–96. *Personalization systems:* Ibid., 133. *Predictions informing stocking and pricing decisions:* Ibid., 204. See also Larry Hardesty, "The History of Amazon's Recommendation Algorithm," Amazon, November 22, 2019.

102, When businesses sell through . . . *"Functions as a . . .":* Lina M. Khan, "Sources of Tech Platform Power," *Georgetown Law Technology Review* 2, no. 2 (2018): 330. See also Dana Mattioli, "Amazon Scooped Up Data from Its Own Sellers to Launch Competing Products," *Wall Street Journal,* April 23, 2020. *"That was something . . .":* Quoted in Stone, *The Everything Store,* 182.

104, This is a surprisingly old idea. *Time-sharing systems:* Tung-Hui Hu, *A Prehistory of the Cloud* (Cambridge, MA: MIT Press, 2015), 37–71, and Devin Kennedy, "The People's Utility," *Logic,* August 1, 2018.

104, The on-demand model . . . *"Computing may someday . . .":* John McCarthy's remarks at the MIT Centennial in 1961, quoted in Simson Garfinkel, *Architects of the Information Society: 35 Years of the Laboratory for Computer Science at MIT* (Cambridge, MA: MIT Press, 1999), 1. *"Information utility":* Martin Greenberger, "The Computers of Tomorrow," *The Atlantic,* May 1964, 63–67.

105, While the modern cloud . . . The cloud symbol was used as early as 1970 in technical diagrams to represent telephone or computer networks; see Hu, *A Prehistory of the Cloud,* x. The first use of the term "cloud computing" in the contemporary sense appears to have been in late 1996, in (eventually abandoned) business plans developed within two companies, Compaq and NetCentric; see Antonio Regalado, "Who Coined 'Cloud Computing'?," *MIT Technology Review,* October 31, 2011.

105, In 2004, an Amazon employee . . . Gareth van Zyl, "Saffer in Silicon Valley, Chris Pinkham, on Being a Top Amazon, Twitter Exec," *BizNews* (South Africa), July 10, 2017; Carl Brooks, "Amazon's Early Efforts at Cloud Computing? Partly Accidental," *TechTarget*, June 17, 2010; and Julie Bort, "Amazon's Game-Changing Cloud Was Built by Some Guys in South Africa," *Business Insider*, March 28, 2012. Pinkham began working at Amazon in January 2001, per LinkedIn.

105, Pinkham and Brown set up shop . . . The first Amazon office in Cape Town was located in the Alphen Office Park. *History of Constantia wine region:* Tim James, *Wines of the New South Africa: Tradition and Revolution* (Berkeley: University of California Press, 2013), 26. *Napoleon ordering bottles of Constantia:* William Forsyth, *History of the Captivity of Napoleon at St. Helena, Volume 2* (New York: Harper and Brothers, 1855), 46. *Cardboard boxes:* The early hire was Roland Paterson-Jones, and his remarks are in Inside Amazon Videos, "Amazon EC2—10 Year Anniversary Celebration," December 8, 2016, YouTube, starts around 1:14. In addition to Pinkham and Brown, the early team in Cape Town included Paterson-Jones, Willem van Biljon, and Quinton Hoole.

106, Pinkham had joined . . . *"Amazon had reached . . .":* Van Zyl, "Saffer in Silicon Valley." *Chaotic internal infrastructure:* John Furrier, "Exclusive: The Story of AWS and Andy Jassy's Trillion Dollar Baby," Medium, January 29, 2015, and Andy Jassy's remarks at AWS Public Sector Summit 2016. *"Jill on the third floor . . .":* Ibid. See also Stone, *The Everything Store*, 211–17 for a discussion of the origins of AWS.

106, So Amazon began . . . In 2002, Bezos instructed all Amazon developers to expose their services through internal APIs. This was also the year the company launched its initial web services effort—then called Amazon.com Web Services—in beta, which gave external developers the ability to incorporate Amazon content and features into their websites. AWS in its mature form began to take shape in 2003. Andy Jassy claims that he finished and presented a vision document for AWS by September 2003, which included a sketch of a compute service. In late 2003, Chris Pinkham and another engineer named Benjamin Black presented a paper that described standardizing Amazon's infrastructure, and included the idea of selling virtual servers as a service. Bezos liked the idea and asked Black to elaborate on it, which he did in a subsequent paper in early 2004. For more on the origins of AWS, see former Amazonian Steve Yegge's (since removed) rant on Google+, available at gist.github.com/chitchcock/1281611; Jeff Barr, "My First 12 Years at Amazon.com," August 19, 2014; Andy Jassy's review of Stone's *The Everything Store* on Amazon.com; Benjamin Black, "EC2 Origins," January 25, 2009; Jack Clark, "How Amazon Exposed Its Guts: The History of AWS's EC2," *ZDNet*, June 7, 2012; Bharath Kumar Gowru et al., "Cloud Computing Using Amazon Web Services," *International Journal for Modern Trends in Science and Technology* 3, no 1 (February 2017): 55; Brandon Butler, "The Myth about How Amazon's Web Service Started Just Won't Die," *NetworkWorld*, March 2, 2015. *"Let's make it . . .":* Jeff Bezos, interview by Om Malik at the D6 Conference in Carlsbad, California, in May 2008, quoted by Nicholas Carr, "Understanding Amazon Web Services," *Rough Type* (blog), May 31, 2008. *Not the only ones feeling the pain:* Furrier, "Exclusive: The Story of AWS and Andy Jassy's Trillion Dollar Baby."

106, The team in Cape Town . . . *Barefoot juggling:* Marcin Kowalski's remarks in "Amazon EC2—10 Year Anniversary Celebration," YouTube, starts around 2:14. *"I spent most . . .":* Quoted in Stone,

The Everything Store, 214. *"It might never . . ."*: Quoted in Brooks, "Amazon's Early Efforts at Cloud Computing? Partly Accidental."

107, The developers in Cape Town . . . Some companies already using virtualization by mid-2000s: In 2001, VMware released ESX, its first "hypervisor" for creating and running virtual machines, which began to be used in data centers.

108, After a year and a half . . . *EC2 launch:* Amazon, "Announcing Amazon Elastic Compute Cloud (Amazon EC2)—beta," August 24, 2006. *S3 launch:* Amazon, "Announcing Amazon S3—Simple Storage Service," March 13, 2006. *Ten cents an hour:* Jeff Barr, "Amazon EC2 Beta," AWS News Blog, August 25, 2006. EC2 launched in 2006 with the m1.small instance, which provided the equivalent of a 1.7 GHz Xeon processor, 1.75 GB of RAM, 160 GB of local disk, and 250 Mb/second of network bandwidth, per ibid. *Market for cloud infrastructure services:* As of Q4 2020, AWS has 32 percent of the global market for cloud infrastructure services, followed by Microsoft Azure at 20 percent and Google Cloud at 9 percent, according to Felix Richter, "Amazon Leads $130-Billion Cloud Market," Statista, February 4, 2021.

108, These dynamics accelerated . . . The 2010s saw the revival of neural networks under the banner of "deep learning," which involves the use of many-layered networks. This revival was made possible by a number of factors, foremost among them advances in computing power and the abundance of training data that could be sourced from the internet. Deep learning is the paradigm that underlies much of what is currently known as "artificial intelligence," and has centrally contributed to significant breakthroughs in computer vision and natural language processing. See Andrey Kurenkov, "A Brief History of Neural Nets and Deep Learning," *Skynet Today*, September 27, 2020, and Alex Hanna et al., "Lines of Sight," *Logic*, December 20, 2020.

109, The sophistication of these systems . . . *"Data imperative"*: Marion Fourcade and Kieran Healy, "Seeing Like a Market," *Socio-Economic Review* 15, no. 1 (2017): 9–29.

110, The same individual . . . *Smartphone usage:* "Mobile Fact Sheet," April 7, 2021, Pew Research Center. In the same period, smartphones proliferated throughout the rest of the world as well: in 2019, the penetration rate reached just over 40 percent of the world's population, some 3.2 billion people.

111, As a kind of networked intelligence . . . *"Be used too:* A. M. Turing, "On Computable Numbers, with an Application to the Entscheidungsproblem," *Proceedings of the London Mathematical Society* 2, no. 1 (1937): 241.

111, What if this universality became ubiquitous? *The network is the computer:* Tekla S. Perry, "Does the Repurposing of Sun Microsystems' Slogan Honor History, or Step on It?," *IEEE Spectrum: View from the Valley,* July 30, 2019.

111, Consider the "smart cooler" . . . *Smart cooler:* Sidney Fussell, "Now Your Groceries See You, Too," *The Atlantic,* January 25, 2019; Lara O'Reilly, "Walgreens Tests Digital Cooler Doors with Cameras to Target You with Ads," *Wall Street Journal,* January 11, 2019.

112, At least, this . . . Lara O'Reilly, "Walgreens Is Expanding Its Digital Cooler Doors Ad Network," *Digiday,* February 3, 2020.

112, But, as with Google . . . *Impossible to determine someone's gender:* Os Keyes, "The Body Instrumental," *Logic,* December 7, 2019. *Geolocation data for ad targeting:* Jennifer Valentino-DeVries et al., "Your Apps Know Where You Were Last Night, and They're Not Keeping It Secret," *New York Times,* December 10, 2018. *Echo smart speaker:* Dorian Lynskey, "'Alexa, Are You Invading My Privacy?'—The Dark Side of Our Voice Assistants," *Guardian,* October 9, 2019; Geoffrey A. Fowler, "Alexa Has Been

Eavesdropping on You This Whole Time," *Washington Post*, May 6, 2019; "The Mystery of the Amazon Echo Data," Privacy International, April 17, 2019.

113, The irony of this phenomenon ... *"The computers have ..."*: Cerf's remarks in Cerf and Kahn, "30th Anniversary of Internetting with TCP/IP," *YouTube*, starts around 11:30.

114, In the late 1970s ... *Fort Bragg demonstration:* Cerf, interview by O'Neill, 29–30. *"Guys would run ..."*: Ibid., 30.

115, No company has fulfilled ... *Uber rates:* uber.com/us/en/ride/.

115, Sometimes this direction ... *The app guides the driver:* Thi Nguyen, "ETA Phone Home: How Uber Engineers an Efficient Route," Uber Engineering, November 3, 2015. *Surge pricing:* Alex Rosenblat and Luke Stark, "Algorithmic Labor and Information Asymmetries: A Case Study of Uber's Drivers," *International Journal of Communication* 10 (2016): 3765–71. *Messages that encourage drivers to keep driving:* Ibid., 3767–69. *Gamified design features:* Sarah Mason, "Chasing the Pink," *Logic*, January 1, 2019.

116, Such techniques would be impossible ... *Surveillance of drivers:* Ibid. and Alex Rosenblat, *Uberland: How Algorithms Are Rewriting the Rules of Work* (Berkeley: University of California Press, 2018), 138–42.

116, Algorithmic management thus enables ... *"In the US ..."*: Veena Dubal, "A Brief History of the Gig," *Logic*, May 4, 2020.

117, Precisely for this reason ... *"Fissured workplace":* David Weil, *The Fissured Workplace: Why Work Became So Bad for So Many and What Can Be Done to Improve It* (Cambridge, MA: Harvard University Press, 2014).

117, Networks are good ... Joan Greenbaum, *Windows on the Workplace: Technology, Jobs, and the Organization of Office Work*, 2nd ed. (New York: Monthly Review Press, 2004 [1995]), 92–94.

117, Networking "supported organizations ..." Ibid., 94.

117, In this respect, the internet . . . Marc Levinson, *The Box: How the Shipping Container Made the World Smaller and the World Economy Bigger* (Princeton: Princeton University Press, 2006).

118, It "has created a massive . . ." *"Has created . . .":* Mueller, *Breaking Things at Work*, 119. *Immense "back office":* Ibid., 117–19, and Mary L. Gray and Siddharth Suri, *Ghost Work: How to Stop Silicon Valley from Building a New Global Underclass* (Boston: Houghton Mifflin, 2019).

119, Uber is one of the main . . . *Singularly unprofitable:* In September 2021, Uber said that it could post its first profit on an adjusted basis in Q3 2021, following a similar announcement by Lyft in the previous quarter. These announcements have more to do with creative accounting than with the health of the underlying businesses, however: the adjusted basis, known as "adjusted EBITDA," excludes many kinds of losses and expenses. As the journalist Preetika Rana notes, "Uber and Lyft have yet to turn a net profit on the strength of their operations and haven't projected when they might." See Preetika Rana, "Uber Says First Adjusted Profit Possible this Quarter," *Wall Street Journal*, September 21, 2021, and Tom McKay, "Uber Says It's on Track to Maybe Make a Fake Profit," *Gizmodo*, September 21, 2021.

120, This was a popular strategy . . . *"The result is . . .":* Srnicek, *Platform Capitalism*, 30. *Profitability numbers:* Jeffrey Funk, "Where Have All the Profitable Startups Gone?," *Mind Matters*, May 27, 2020.

121, The data has both an operational . . . *"Attracts venture capital . . .":* Niels van Doorn and Adam Badger, "Platform Capitalism's Hidden Abode: Producing Data Assets in the Gig Economy," *Antipode* 52, no. 5 (2020): 1477.

121, Whether this growth will . . . *"One of the greatest . . ." and First Round Capital:* Scott Austin, Stephanie Stamm, and Rolfe Winkler,

"Uber Jackpot: Inside One of the Greatest Startup Investments of All Time," *Wall Street Journal*, May 10, 2019. *Goldman Sachs:* Wilfred Frost and Hugh Son, "Goldman Sachs Dumped Its Entire Stake in Uber Late Last Year," CNBC, January 15, 2020. *Travis Kalanick:* Eliot Brown, "Uber Co-Founder Travis Kalanick Cuts Stake in Company by More Than 90%," *Wall Street Journal*, December 21, 2019.

122, Just because Uber is . . . For data on the growing GDP share of the financial industry, see Thomas Philippon, "Has the U.S. Finance Industry Become Less Efficient? On the Theory and Measurement of Financial Intermediation," *American Economic Review* 105, no. 4 (2015): 1408–38.

123, These companies were so successful . . . *Facebook acquisitions:* Mark Glick and Catherine Ruetschlin, "Big Tech Acquisitions and the Potential Competition Doctrine: The Case of Facebook," *Institute for New Economic Thinking Working Paper Series* 104 (2019): 57–60. *Google acquisitions:* CB Insights, "The Google Acquisition Tracker," available at cbinsights.com/.

124, Moreover, there aren't . . . *Decline in GDP and labor productivity growth rates:* Aaron Benanav, *Automation and the Future of Work* (London: Verso, 2020), 31–32; Robert Brenner, *The Economics of Global Turbulence: The Advanced Capitalist Economies from Long Boom to Long Downturn, 1945–2005* (Verso: London, 2018 [2006]), 341. *Richest .01 percent of Americans quintupling their share of national wealth:* Howard R. Gold, "Never Mind the 1 Percent. Let's Talk about the 0.01 Percent," *Chicago Booth Review* (Winter 2017).

8. Inclusive Predators

126, Doug Schifter spent more . . . Jessica Bruder, "Driven to Despair," *New York Magazine*, May 14, 2018; Ginia Bellafante, "A

Driver's Suicide Reveals the Dark Side of the Gig Economy," *New York Times*, February 6, 2018.

126, He wanted his suicide . . . Schifter's columns are available at drivingguild.org/doug-schifter-black-car-news-column-archive/. *"Due to the huge numbers . . .":* Schifter's suicide note, available at imgur.com/gallery/M24BM. The original has been deleted by Facebook.

128, Take Uber. Dubal, "A Brief History of the Gig."

130, In his suicide note . . . *"Limited competition":* Schifter's suicide note, available at https://imgur.com/gallery/M24BM. Taxi regulations won through collective action: Dubal, "A Brief History of the Gig."

130, Uber's arrival changed that. *"Now there are . . .":* Ibid.

130, The upshot, as Schifter predicted . . . A number of studies have shown that ride-hail drivers earn less than the mandated minimum wage in their local markets. A 2018 report found that drivers' "W-2 equivalent hourly wage falls below the mandated minimum wage in the majority of major Uber urban markets (13 of 20 major markets, which include 18 cities, a county, and a state)"; see Lawrence Mishel, "Uber and the Labor Market," Economic Policy Institute, May 15, 2018. A 2020 report prepared for the city of Seattle found that drivers earned less than the minimum wage in Seattle; see James A. Parrott and Michael Reich, "A Minimum Compensation Standard for Seattle TNC Drivers," Center for New York City Affairs at The New School, July 2020. A 2018 report by the same team found that drivers also earned less than the minimum wage in New York City: James A. Parrott and Michael Reich, "An Earnings Standard for New York City's App-Based Drivers," Center for New York City Affairs at The New School, July 2018. (In December 2018, legislation passed to ensure that New York City's ride-hail drivers earn a minimum wage of

$17.22 an hour after expenses.) Finally, a 2020 study found that drivers in San Francisco earned less than the minimum wage: Chris Benner et al., "On-Demand and On-the-Edge: Ride-hailing and Delivery Workers in San Francisco," UC Santa Cruz Institute for Social Transformation, May 20, 2020. *Georgetown study:* Katie J. Wells, Kafui Attoh, and Declan Cullen, "The Uber Workplace in DC," Georgetown University Kalmanovitz Initiative for Labor and the Working Poor, April 2019.

130, Inspired by Uber's example . . . *"Uberization":* Alexis Madrigal and his colleagues at *The Atlantic* assembled a spreadsheet of 105 "Uber-for-X" companies. *Prop 22 campaign and pursuit of similar measures:* Josh Eidelson, "The Gig Economy Is Coming for Millions of American Jobs," *Bloomberg Businessweek*, February 17, 2021, and Kate Conger, "Gig Companies Want Massachusetts Voters to Exempt Workers from Employee Status," *New York Times*, August 4, 2021. Judge's ruling against Prop 22: Kate Conger and Kellen Browning, "A Judge Declared California's Gig Worker Law Unconstitutional. Now What?," *New York Times*, August 23, 2021. *Carolan op-ed:* Shawn Carolan, "What Proposition 22 Now Makes Possible," *The Information*, November 10, 2020. *Albertsons:* Eidelson, "The Gig Economy Is Coming." *"It is too late . . .":* Schifter's suicide note, available at imgur.com/gallery/M24BM.

131, For every worker . . . According to the staffing agency directory OnContracting, contingent labor accounts for 40 to 50 percent of the workforce at most tech firms; see Daisuke Wakabayashi, "Google's Shadow Work Force: Temps Who Outnumber Full-Time Employees," *New York Times*, May 18, 2019. Google is especially reliant on contingent labor; the company has more temps, vendors, and contractors (TVCs) than full-time employees.

131, They also perform . . . Gray and Suri, *Ghost Work*.

132, This shadow workforce is just . . . A 2016 report found that average earnings for direct employees in Silicon Valley was $113,300, while white-collar contract workers made $53,200 and blue-collar contract workers made $19,900. The same study found that contract workers receive few benefits: 31 percent of blue-collar contract workers had no health insurance at all. See Silicon Valley Rising, "Tech's Invisible Workforce," March 2016. *Traumatizing working conditions for content moderators:* Sarah T. Roberts, *Behind the Screen: Content Moderation in the Shadows of Social Media* (New Haven, CT: Yale University Press, 2019).

132, Predatory inclusion, argues . . . *Predatory inclusion:* Tressie McMillan Cottom, "Where Platform Capitalism and Racial Capitalism Meet: The Sociology of Race and Racism in the Digital Society," *Sociology of Race and Ethnicity* 6, no. 4 (2020): 441–49. *"The logic, organization . . .":* Ibid., 443.

133, This is a common pattern . . . The inclusion of the excluded is often a point emphasized by tech companies themselves. For example, Sama, a company that recruits data-annotation workers from the slums of the Global South, presents its business in humanitarian terms; see Mueller, *Breaking Things at Work*, 118–19. The advertising materials in the campaign for Proposition 22 struck a similar note, promoting the narrative that gig companies offer economic opportunities to Black and Latino workers; see Levi Sumagaysay, "Race Has Played a Large Role in Uber and Lyft's Fight to Preserve Their Business Models," *MarketWatch*, October 19, 2020.

133, On a spring morning . . . Noble, *Algorithms of Oppression*, 17.

134, In the 1990s, the idea . . . *Television commercials:* Lisa Nakamura, *Cybertypes: Race, Ethnicity, and Identity on the Internet* (New York: Routledge, 2002), 87–99. *Prominent pundits:* Ibid., 13, 106–7. *"Ours is a world . . .":* Barlow, "A Declaration of the Independence of Cyberspace."

134, Yet it was abundantly clear . . . *"It wasn't a question . . .":* Charlton McIlwain, *Black Software: The Internet and Racial Justice, From the Afronet to Black Lives Matter* (Oxford: Oxford University Press, 2020), 96. See ibid., 95–97, for a discussion of racism on Usenet. There is also the notorious case discussed by journalist Julian Dibbell in his piece "A Rape in Cyberspace," initially published in the *Village Voice* in December 1993 and later included in revised form in *My Tiny Life: Crime and Passion in a Virtual World* (New York: Henry Holt and Company, 1998). *"Racial enlightenment":* Quoted in Jessie Daniels, *Cyber Racism: White Supremacy Online and the New Attack on Civil Rights* (Lanham, MD: Rowman & Littlefield, 2009), 3. Daniels's book offers a thorough discussion of the rise of the white-supremacist internet.

134, The fact that oppression . . . *"Images of race . . .":* Nakamura, *Cybertypes*, 15. *"Preserves the . . .":* Ibid., 18.

136, At first, the algorithms . . . Google does not disclose the inner workings of its search algorithms, but it does publish guidance on SEO for site owners; see developers.google.com/search/docs.

136, The search engine examines . . . *It no longer does:* Noble noticed the change after she published an article about her experience in *Bitch* magazine in 2012; see Noble, *Algorithms of Oppression*, 181. *"Unprofessional hairstyles . . .":* Ibid., 82–83. As of June 2021, a Google search for "unprofessional hairstyles for work" surfaces content from a number of articles about racist search results, including from the *Guardian* and the *Telegraph*.

136, This is what cybertyping . . . On the subject of "increased visibility," see Noble's analysis of algorithmic hypervisibility in Noble, "Google Search: Hyper-visibility as a Means of Rendering Black Women and Girls Invisible," *InVisible Culture* 19 (October 2013).

137, Ideologies like racism . . . *"Must be constantly . . .":* Barbara J. Fields, "Slavery, Race, and Ideology in the United States of

America," in Barbara J. Fields and Karen E. Fields, *Racecraft: The Soul of Inequality in American Life* (London: Verso, 2014 [2012]), 137. *Facebook's ad portal investigated:* Tracy Jan and Elizabeth Dwoskin, "HUD Is Reviewing Twitter's and Google's Ad Practices as Part of Housing Discrimination Probe," *Washington Post*, March 28, 2019; American Civil Liberties Union, "Facebook Agrees to Sweeping Reforms to Curb Discriminatory Ad Practices," March 19, 2019.

137, But discrimination persists. *Use of proxies and algorithmic contributions:* Ava Kofman and Ariana Tobin, "Facebook Ads Can Still Discriminate against Women and Older Workers, despite a Civil Rights Settlement," ProPublica, December 13, 2019. *Northeastern, USC, and Upturn study:* Muhammad Ali et al., "Discrimination through Optimization: How Facebook's Ad Delivery Can Lead to Biased Outcomes," *Proceedings of the ACM on Human-Computer Interaction* 3, no. CSCW (November 2019): 1–30. See also Basileal Imana, Aleksandra Korolova, and John Heidemann, "Auditing for Discrimination in Algorithms Delivering Job Ads," in *Proceedings of the Web Conference 2021* (New York: ACM, 2021), 3767–78. There is also evidence that Facebook advertisers can still target financial product ads to particular age groups; see Corin Faife and Alfred Ng, "Credit Cards Ads Were Targeted by Age, Violating Facebook's Anti-discrimination Policy," *The Markup*, April 29, 2021.

138, In 2015, a neo-Nazi . . . Noble, *Algorithms of Oppression*, 111. The Southern Poverty Law Center labels the Council of Conservative Citizens a white-nationalist and white-supremacist hate group.

138, Roof's fateful encounter . . . "The first website I came to was the Council of Conservative Citizens," Roof writes in his manifesto, although it's unknown exactly where the CCC site appeared in the ranking of search results. See Rebecca Hersher, "What Happened When Dylann Roof Asked Google for Information about Race," NPR, January 10, 2017.

139, Online malls are inequality machines . . . *"New old regime"*:
Corey Robin, *The Reactionary Mind* (Oxford: Oxford University
Press, 2011), 43.

139, Seeing conservatives as radicals . . . *"Innovation opportunists"*:
Jessie Daniels, "The Algorithmic Rise of the 'Alt-Right,'" *Contexts*
17, no. 1 (2018): 63.

140, Polarization is a good place . . . *"Increased the most . . ."*: Levi
Boxell, Matthew Gentzkow, and Jesse M. Shapiro, "Greater Inter-
net Use Is Not Associated with Faster Growth in Political
Polarization among US Demographic Groups," *Proceedings of the
National Academy of Sciences* 114, no. 40 (October 3, 2017): 10616.
See also Levi Boxell, Matthew Gentzkow, and Jesse M. Shapiro,
"Cross-Country Trends in Affective Polarization," National Bureau
of Economic Research, 2020, and Yochai Benkler, Robert Faris,
and Hal Roberts, *Network Propaganda: Manipulation, Disinforma-
tion, and Radicalization in American Politics* (Oxford: Oxford
University Press, 2018), 296–339.

141, But the Right has immeasurably . . . The journalist Kevin
Roose compiles the ten top-performing link posts by public US
Facebook pages every day and publishes them on Twitter at twitter.
com/FacebooksTop10. Partly in an attempt to rebut Roose's work,
Facebook began publishing a quarterly report on "widely viewed
content" in August 2021 that claims to offer a more comprehensive
view, given the fact that link posts are a relatively small percentage
of the content seen by Facebook users as a whole. But journalists
and scholars have criticized these reports for their lack of transpar-
ency and, given the company's long record of misleading the
public, it seems likely that the information is being carefully
framed to present the company in a positive light. See Will
Oremus, "Facebook Shared New Data about What's Popular on Its
Platform. The Answers Are Deeply Weird," *Washington Post*,

August 18, 2021, and Shoshana Wodinsky, "Facebook's 'Widely Viewed Content' Report Promises Ben Shapiro Isn't That Popular," *Gizmodo*, August 18, 2021.

141, What's more, it is figures . . . *NYU study:* Laura Edelson et al., "Far-Right News Sources on Facebook More Engaging," Cyber-security for Democracy, March 3, 2021. *No measurable effect from Russian influence operations:* Benkler, Faris, and Roberts, *Network Propaganda*, 235–68, and Yochai Benkler, "Cautionary Notes on Disinformation and the Origins of Distrust," *MediaWell*, October 22, 2019. *"Mostly took the . . .":* Yochai Benkler, "The Danger of Overstating the Impact of Information Operations," *Lawfare*, October 23, 2020.

142, These forces have . . . *Right-wing media ecosystem:* Benkler, Faris, and Roberts, *Network Propaganda*, 75–99. *Fox as most-viewed US cable network:* Amy Watson, "Top Cable News Networks U.S. 2021, by Number of Viewers," Statista, June 7, 2021. *Fox as one of the most popular US publishers on Facebook:* Benedict Nicholson, "These Were the Top Publishers on Facebook in November 2020," *NewsWhip*, December 9, 2020. *"Trading up the chain":* Alice Marwick and Rebecca Lewis, "Media Manipulation and Disinformation Online," Data & Society Research Institute, May 15, 2017.

142, This messiness is manifest . . . *Lack of evidence for "filter bubbles":* Peter M. Dahlgren, "A Critical Review of Filter Bubbles and a Comparison with Selective Exposure," *Nordicom Review* 42, no. 1 (2021): 15–33; Axel Bruns, "Filter Bubble," *Internet Policy Review* 8, no. 4 (2019). *"Widespread heterogeneity . . .":* P. M. Krafft and Joan Donovan, "Disinformation by Design: The Use of Evidence Collages and Platform Filtering in a Media Manipulation Campaign," *Political Communication* 37, no. 2 (2020): 195. *"An arsenal of tactics":* Ibid., 196.

143, **This is not to deny . . .** *Research within Facebook:* Hao, "How Facebook Got Addicted to Spreading Misinformation." In some parts of the world, the algorithmic favoring of provocative content has contributed to atrocities: in Myanmar, propaganda distributed on Facebook by ethnonationalist extremists helped incite genocidal violence against the Rohingya Muslim minority. See the United Nations Human Rights Council's Independent International Fact-Finding Mission on Myanmar report from 2018.

144, **But the code that determines . . .** *Different kinds of engagement:* Zuckerberg's January 2018 announcement that Facebook would begin prioritizing "time well spent," available at facebook.com/ zuck/posts/10104413015393571. For an analysis of "time well spent" as a new attention-monetization strategy, see Ben Tarnoff and Moira Weigel, "Why Silicon Valley Can't Fix Itself," *Guardian*, May 3, 2018. According to internal Facebook documents reviewed by the *Wall Street Journal*, the 2018 algorithm change inspired by the "time well spent" strategy actually increased the amount of sensationalist content on the site; see Keach Hagey and Jeff Horwitz, "Facebook Tried to Make Its Platform a Healthier Place. It Got Angrier Instead," *Wall Street Journal*, September 15, 2021. In 2020, Facebook had 15,000 content moderation workers, the vast majority of them subcontractors; in 2016, it only had 4,500 such workers. See Paul M. Barrett, "Who Moderates the Social Media Giants? A Call to End Outsourcing," NYU Stern Center for Business and Human Rights, June 2020, 4, 8. The same report states that during the COVID-19 pandemic, Facebook came to rely more heavily on automated systems for content moderation. *Strategies developed by reactionaries for YouTube:* Rebecca Lewis, "Alternative Influence: Broadcasting the Reactionary Right on YouTube," Data & Society Research Institute, September 18, 2018.

145, The online malls . . . Félix Guattari, "The Three Ecologies,"
trans. Chris Turner, *New Formations* 8 (Summer 1989): 131–47.

145, While this relationship is mutually . . . *Facebook crackdown on
Stop the Steal group and internal report:* Craig Silverman, Ryan
Mac, and Jane Lytvynenko, "Facebook Knows It Was Used to
Help Incite the Capitol Insurrection," *BuzzFeed News*, April 22,
2021; Ryan Mac, Craig Silverman, and Jane Lytvynenko, "Facebook Stopped Employees from Reading an Internal Report about
Its Role in the Insurrection. You Can Read It Here," *BuzzFeed
News*, April 26, 2021. *Facebook made a lot of money from QAnon:*
Matt Stoller estimates that Facebook made nearly $3 billion from
QAnon in 2020, based on a rough calculation of the number of
QAnon-sympathetic users; see Matt Stoller, "Facebook Made Up to
$2.9 billion from QAnon in 2020," March 22, 2021. *Not particularly effective ban:* QAnon continues to be active on Facebook,
according to a report by US nonprofit Avaaz, "Facebook: From
Election to Insurrection," March 18, 2021.

146, These measures are motivated . . . *"Advertisers don't want . . .":*
Nick Clegg, "You and the Algorithm: It Takes Two to Tango,"
March 31, 2021.

146, Making the balancing act . . . *Zuckerberg currying favor with
Republican leaders and the latter's influence on content policies:*
Natasha Bertrand and Daniel Lippman, "Inside Mark Zuckerberg's
Private Meetings with Conservative Pundits," *Politico*, October 14,
2019; Craig Timberg, "How Conservatives Learned to Wield
Power inside Facebook," *Washington Post*, February 20, 2020;
Elizabeth Dwoskin, Craig Timberg, and Tony Romm, "Zuckerberg Once Wanted to Sanction Trump. Then Facebook Wrote
Rules That Accommodated Him," *Washington Post*, June 28, 2020.
Kaplan's interventions: Hao, "How Facebook Got Addicted to
Spreading Misinformation"; Deepa Seetharaman, "Facebook's

Lonely Conservative Takes on a Power Position," *Wall Street Journal*, December 23, 2018; Jeff Horwitz and Deepa Seetharaman, "Facebook Executives Shut Down Efforts to Make the Site Less Divisive," *Wall Street Journal*, May 26, 2020.

9. Toward the Forest

148, The soundtrack to the privatization . . . *"The Teflon industry":* Rana Foroohar, "Year in a Word: Techlash," *Financial Times*, December 16, 2018.

148, At some point . . . The *Financial Times* called "techlash" one of 2018's words of the year; it was also a runner-up for the Oxford Dictionary's 2018 word of the year. Google Trends, a tool that displays the popularity of search queries over time, confirms that the word first caught on in 2018.

149, As the years have passed . . . *Polling:* Carroll Doherty and Jocelyn Kiley, "Americans Have Become Much Less Positive about Tech Companies' Impact on the U.S.," Pew Research Center, July 29, 2019.

149, This doesn't mean . . . *Priorities largely set by corporations and the rich:* Martin Gilens and Benjamin I. Page, "Testing Theories of American Politics: Elites, Interest Groups, and Average Citizens," *Perspectives on Politics* 12, no. 3 (2014): 564–81. Gilens and Page's research found that "economic elites and organized groups representing business interests have substantial independent impacts on U.S. government policy, while average citizens and mass-based interest groups have little or no independent influence."

150, The second trend aims . . . My description of the New Brandeisians in this section draws from Lina Khan, "The New Brandeis Movement: America's Antimonopoly Debate," *Journal of European Competition Law and Practice* 9, no. 3 (2018): 131–32; Tim Wu, *The Curse of Bigness: Antitrust in the New Gilded Age* (New York:

Columbia Global Reports, 2018); and Barry Lynn, *Cornered: The New Monopoly Capitalism and the Economics of Destruction* (New York: Wiley, 2009). See also Tim Wu, "The Utah Statement: Reviving Antimonopoly Traditions for the Era of Big Tech," *OneZero*, November 18, 2019.

150, Toward this end . . . *Proposal for forcing Facebook to spin off WhatsApp:* Barry Lynn and Matt Stoller, "Facebook Must Be Restructured. The FTC Should Take These Nine Steps Now," *Guardian*, March 22, 2018. The antitrust lawsuits filed by the FTC and forty-eight state attorneys general in December 2020—and dismissed by a federal judge in June 2021—also called for such a move.

150, Their advocacy is having . . . *House Judiciary report:* US House Judiciary Subcommittee on Antitrust, Commercial, and Administrative Law, "Investigation of Competition in Digital Markets," October 6, 2020. *Justice Department antitrust suit:* Department of Justice, "Justice Department Sues Monopolist Google for Violating Antitrust Laws," October 20, 2020. *Biden's executive order:* "Executive Order on Promoting Competition in the American Economy," July 9, 2021. The FTC antitrust suit was dismissed by a federal court on June 28, 2021; the agency subsequently refiled the suit in August 2021.

151, Each strain of internet . . . Khan, "The New Brandeis Movement," 132.

152, But would it? *"After all . . .":* Nick Srnicek, "The Only Way to Rein In Big Tech Is to Treat Them as a Public Service," *Guardian*, April 23, 2019. *"Lead to yet . . .":* The Ezra Klein Show, "Facebook Is a Capitalism Problem, Not a Mark Zuckerberg Problem," *Vox: Recode*, May 10, 2019. *Hundreds of millions of dollars on content moderation:* Deepa Seetharaman, "Facebook Throws More Money at Wiping Out Hate Speech and Bad Actors," *Wall Street Journal*, May 15, 2018.

154, A privatized internet . . . As of May 2021, Zuckerberg controls about 58 percent of the voting shares of Facebook; see Naomi Nix, "Facebook Board Rejects Proposals to Curb Zuckerberg's Power," *Bloomberg*, May 26, 2021. Changes to the board of directors in recent years have also consolidated Zuckerberg's power over the company; see Deepa Seetharaman and Emily Glazer, "Mark Zuckerberg Asserts Control of Facebook, Pushing Aside Dissenters," *Wall Street Journal*, April 28, 2020.

156, This position often invites . . . Angela Davis, interview by Amy Goodman, *Democracy Now!*, July 3, 2020, transcript available at democracynow.org.

156, To do so, Davis argues . . . *"Let go of . . .":* Angela Davis, *Are Prisons Obsolete?* (New York: Seven Stories Press, 2003), 106. *"Constellation . . .":* Ibid., 107. *"Lay claim . . .":* Ibid., 107–8.

157, What might some . . . Sarah T. Hamid, interview by *Logic*, "Community Defense: Sarah T. Hamid on Abolishing Carceral Technologies," *Logic*, August 31, 2020.

157, Abolishing the online malls . . . Ruha Benjamin, *Race After Technology* (Cambridge: Polity, 2019), 168.

158, Instead of Facebook . . . *"Plural . . ."* and *"Pool halls . . .":* Ethan Zuckerman, "What Is Digital Public Infrastructure?," Center for Journalism and Liberty, November 17, 2020.

158, But bigness "makes . . ." *"Makes true . . ."* and *"A 'community' . . .":* Ibid.

160, Mastodon is not tiny. "Decentralized web" is an expansive term and includes many projects that have little social value. For more about the ideas that are guiding the community's progressive currents, see the DWeb Principles at getdweb.net.

160, The United States has more . . . *"Had a federated . . ."* and *"If your . . .":* Darius Kazemi, interview by *Logic*, "Party at My House: Darius Kazemi on Human-Scaled Social Media," *Logic*, May 4, 2020.

160, Libraries have a further . . . *"Our knowledge needs":* Noble, *Algorithms of Oppression,* 16. For data on declining funding for public libraries, see Institute of Museum and Library Services, *Public Libraries in the United States: Fiscal Year 2017,* vol. 1 (Washington, DC: The Institute, 2020). *"Building systems . . .":* Joan Donovan, "Hire 10,000 Librarians for the Internet," in Julia Carrie Wong, "Banning Trump Won't Fix Social Media: 10 Ideas to Rebuild Our Broken Internet—by Experts," *Guardian,* January 16, 2021.

161, The problems that librarians . . . *"Profit motives drive . . .":* Victor Pickard, *Democracy without Journalism? Confronting the Misinformation Society* (Oxford: Oxford University Press, 2019), 11. The death of the Fairness Doctrine at the hands of the Reagan administration in 1987 proved to be an especially useful deregulatory move for right-wing media; see Kevin M. Kruse and Julian Zelizer, "How Policy Decisions Spawned Today's Hyperpolarized Media," *Washington Post,* January 17, 2019. *Donor-subsidized right-wing sites:* Alex Pareene, "Liberals Are Losing the Journalism Wars," *New Republic,* October 21, 2020.

161, Commercial media's failings . . . *"Permanent trust . . .":* Pickard, *Democracy without Journalism?,* 156. *"Community media centers":* Ibid., 157.

162, Much of what circulates . . . *"Present a wider . . ." and "More critical . . .":* Ibid., 159–60.

162, Another way to think . . . *Content moderation as care work:* Lindsay Bartkowski, "Caring for the Internet: Content Moderators and the Maintenance of Empire," *Journal of Working-Class Studies* 4, no. 1 (June 2019): 66–78. *"Racialized workers . . ." and "Affinities . . .":* Ibid., 67.

163, A social media that is . . . *Fediverse response to Gab:* Adi Robertson, "How the Biggest Decentralized Social Network Is Dealing with Its Nazi Problem," *The Verge*, July 12, 2019. *"Decision making . . ."*: Mike Masnick, "Protocols, Not Platforms: A Technological Approach to Free Speech," Knight First Amendment Institute, August 21, 2019.

163, Social media is only . . . *"Ensures privacy . . ."*: Nick Srnicek, "The Only Way to Rein In Big Tech Is to Treat Them as a Public Service," *Guardian*, April 23, 2019.

164, This sector would include . . . *Up & Go:* Michaela Haas, "'When Someone Hires Me, They Get the Boss Herself,'" *New York Times*, July 7, 2020; Ilana Novick, "Cleaning Workers Are Fighting for Better Pay and Benefits," *Vice*, August 8, 2018; Eillie Anzilotti, "Up and Go Is a Worker-Owned Alternative to On-Demand Home Cleaning Services," *Fast Company*, May 16, 2017. *"Cooperativism . . ."*: Marve Romero, interview by Ana Ulin, "Issue 9: Tech Work under the Pandemic—Cleaner and App Co-Owner," *TWC Newsletter*, April 1, 2021.

164, Similar efforts exist . . . The "Platform Co-op Directory" maintained by the Platform Cooperativism Consortium lists 504 projects in thirty-three countries; see directory.platform.coop/. For more on platform cooperativism, see Trebor Scholz and Nathan Schneider, eds., *Ours to Hack and Own: The Rise of Platform Cooperativism, a New Vision for the Future of Work and a Fairer Internet* (New York: OR Books, 2016); Nathan Schneider, *Everything for Everyone: The Radical Tradition That Is Shaping the Next Economy* (New York: PublicAffairs, 2018). *Municipal regulatory codes:* Seth Ackerman, "How to Socialize Uber," *Jacobin*, April 7, 2015. Ackerman cites several precedents for such restrictions: "Many states forbid corporations from engaging in certain kinds of farming; many exclude for-profit companies from certain kinds of gambling and credit counseling businesses; and federal restrictions on foreign ownership exist in a wide range of industries."

Uber's 2017 London suspension: Prashant S. Rao and Mike Isaac, "Uber Loses License to Operate in London," *New York Times*, September 22, 2017. *Cooperatively owned taxi idea:* "New Economics Foundation Calls for 'Khan's Cars' as Mutually Owned Alternative to Uber," New Economics Foundation, September 22, 2017.

165, Then there is . . . Salomé Viljoen, "Democratic Data: A Relational Theory for Data Governance," 2020.

165, Data is made collectively . . . *"To shape . . .":* Ibid., 54. *Malmgren's proposal:* Evan Malmgren, "Socialized Media," *The Baffler*, September 19, 2018.

167, An interesting model . . . Michael Rustin, "Lessons of the London Industrial Strategy," *New Left Review* 155 (January/February 1986): 75–84.

167, It also established five . . . My discussion of the Technology Networks in this section draws from Adrian Smith, "Technology Networks for Socially Useful Production," *Journal of Peer Production* 5 (2014): 1–9 and Greater London Enterprise Board, *Technology Networks: Science and Technology Serving London's Needs* (London: GLEB, 1984), available at grassrootsinnovations.files.wordpress.com/2014/04/gleb-1984-technology-networks.pdf.

167, One purpose of these spaces . . . *"Making sure . . .":* Quoted in Smith, "Technology Networks for Socially Useful Production," 3.

169, For such efforts . . . *"We believe that everyone . . .":* "Design Justice Network Principles," available at designjustice.org/read-the-principles. *"Nothing about us . . .":* Sasha Costanza-Chock, *Design Justice: Community-Led Practices to Build the Worlds We Need* (Cambridge, MA: MIT Press, 2020), 93.

170, One way to do so . . . *"Adversarial interoperability":* Cory Doctorow, "Adversarial Interoperability: Reviving an Elegant Weapon from a More Civilized Age to Slay Today's Monopolies," Electronic

Frontier Foundation, June 7, 2019; Cory Doctorow, "Adversarial Interoperability," Electronic Frontier Foundation, October 2, 2019. Some proposed legislation that would require social media companies to implement a degree of interoperability is the ACCESS Act of 2019 (S. 2658) and the ACCESS Act of 2021 (H.R. 3849).

170, But going on the offensive . . . Smith, "Technology Networks for Socially Useful Production," 5.

Conclusion: Future Nostalgia

172, On the early internet . . . *"The imminent death of the net . . .":* Eric S. Raymond and Guy L. Steele, eds., *The New Hacker's Dictionary,* 3rd ed. (Cambridge, MA: MIT Press, 1996 [1983]), 254.

172, The nostalgics are no . . . *"Culture of serendipitous tinkering":* Jonathan Zittrain, "The Internet Is Closing to Innovation," *Newsweek,* November 28, 2008. *A gritty, eccentric metropolis:* Virginia Heffernan, "The Death of the Open Web," *New York Times,* May 21, 2010. For more in this vein, see also Dries Buytaert, "Can We Save the Open Web?," March 16, 2016.

173, Nostalgia never paints . . . *"Asymmetrical power . . .":* Anja Bechmann, "Internet Profiling: The Economy of Data Interoperability on Facebook and Google," *MedieKultur: Journal of Media and Communication Research* 29, no. 55 (2013): 75. See also Helmond, "The Platformization of the Web," and David B. Nieborg and Anne Helmond, "The Political Economy of Facebook's Platformization in the Mobile Ecosystem: Facebook Messenger as a Platform Instance," *Media, Culture and Society* 41, no. 2 (2019): 196–218.

173, As for whether the result . . . *Black Twitter:* André Brock Jr., *Distributed Blackness: African American Cybercultures* (New York: New York University Press, 2020), 79–124.

174, In his history of the English . . . For Luddite literature, see Kevin Binfield, ed., *Writings of the Luddites* (Baltimore: Johns Hopkins University Press, 2004). *"Industrial growth . . .":* E. P. Thompson, *The Making of the English Working Class* (New York: Vintage Books, 1966 [1963]), 552.

Index